Wicked Pissed

WICKED PISSED

New England's Most Famous Feuds

TED REINSTEIN

Globe
Pequot

Guilford, Connecticut

(handwritten: 1/19/17)

(handwritten: To Nancy)

(handwritten signature: Best, Ted)

Globe
Pequot

An imprint of Rowman & Littlefield

Distributed by NATIONAL BOOK NETWORK

British Library Cataloguing in Publication Information Available

Library of Congress Cataloging-in-Publication Data

ISBN 978-1-4930-0887-2 (paperback)
ISBN 978-1-4930-2332-5 (e-book)

∞™ The paper used in this publication meets the minimum requirements of American National Standard for Information Sciences—Permanence of Paper for Printed Library Materials, ANSI/ NISO Z39.48-1992.

For Anne-Marie, Kyra, and Daisy
For Your Continued Love and Support

Contents

Preface

(Can't We All Just Get Along?)

In Massachusetts, lawyers and judges still marvel at the most expensive civil suit in the state's history.

It spanned decades, cost hundreds of millions, and had a cast of characters like a Russian novel. No one was killed or injured. No product was at fault. The plaintiffs were, in fact, very well-acquainted with each other. After all, they were family. It was business. And nothing will split up a family faster than a wayward blade that seems to be carving up the profits unfairly. The legal marathon was merely the outward, public manifestation of a seething, bitter, relentless family feud that would ultimately snare twenty-five thousand others in the middle of it, bring a booming and successful business to its knees, and make international news.

In Vermont, they still have the striking home that Rudyard Kipling built high on a hill. They'd rather have had a long line of Kipling descendants still calling the Green Mountains home. Alas, when Kipling left Vermont, he was never to come back. A very ugly, very public dispute with a brother-in-law will do that.

Only one state in America doesn't automatically answer "the Wright brothers" to the question, "Who was first in flight?" And in Connecticut, they will be happy to take it up—as they have for decades—with North Carolina, the Smithsonian, and anyone else who'd care to listen to their side of what's become a serious spat about who deserves aviation's greatest honor.

Let's face it: Feuds fascinate. They always have. As long as they're not ours.

The Bible is full of feuds. (Cain and Abel, anyone?) The perpetually warring city-states of antiquity were rife with them. (Athens and Sparta ring a bell?) Consider just the literature that feuds have inspired. Without them, Shakespeare would have had half the material to work with. With them, we have *Hamlet, King Lear,* and *Romeo and Juliet.* Not to mention the unending feud between those who think that Shakespeare actually *wrote* those plays and those who don't.

World history and relations between nations have forever hinged (and become unhinged) because of feuds. England versus France. Spain versus England. Russia versus everyone.

Our own American history is no exception, with bitter and festering feuds from the start. And in the case of Native Americans and the European newcomers, it's never really ended.

Consider that America's very first secretary of the treasury, Alexander Hamilton, incensed by a longtime rival, was shot and killed in a *duel*, for goodness sake. (That must have made for a somewhat subdued subsequent cabinet meeting.)

What was the American Revolution, after all, if not the nation's founding feud? And less than a century afterward, what was the American Civil War, if not the most horrific of family feuds? Indeed, it was the Civil War that later gave rise to a bitter feud between two actual families on either side of the border dividing Kentucky and

West Virginia. Today, "like the Hatfields and McCoys" has entered the American lexicon to describe fierce feuding of any kind.

The early days of the American West spawned some legendary feuds. (It wasn't a cookout at the OK Corral.) The rise of the railroads, cattle, land, oil barons, unions, Hollywood, the whole sweep of American politics—filled with feuds.

Then there's New England.

Too far north to be a flashpoint for returning Civil War vets nursing murderous grudges against their neighbors (the original DNA of the Hatfield/McCoy feud). No oil, and too small for the land battles or cattle wars of the wide-open west. Fierce feuds between fading stars and upstart ingénues? That's for Tinseltown, not Tilton, Topsham, or Tunbridge.

No, New England's famous feuds and disputed claims have been different: older, often rooted in history, as colorful, varied, and unique as the region's diverse people and landscape itself, and as surprising and changeable as the region's famously unpredictable weather.

From the rugged woods of the Canadian border, to Connecticut's bedroom communities for Manhattan, from the mountains to its islands offshore, New England's feuds have peppered the region's life for centuries. From sports to politics, food to finance, aviation to engineering, to bitter disputes over simple boundaries themselves, New England has seen feuds pitting people from every walk of life imaginable against each other. Sure, New England has produced nation founders, marvels of invention, magnificent universities and medical institutions, as well as masters of music, art, and literature. But it sure has produced some memorable feuds, too.

Nor have New Englanders been shy about feuding across state (and regional) lines. Consider Connecticut's nasty spat with North Carolina over the Wright brothers' legacy. Ask them in Holliston,

Massachusetts, where the real Mudville of "Casey at the Bat" fame is. Then mention Stockton, California. And stand back. Even green and crunchy, "it's all good" Vermont—New England's most laid-back, live-and-let-live state—has managed to find itself in a silly, snarky snit with *Arizona*, of all places. Go figure, dude.

They've been raw and rowdy, sometimes high-minded and humorous, and in a place renowned for its deep sense of history, often long-running and legendary. There are feuds in New England that will undoubtedly outlast the region's ancient low stone walls.

In New England nothing says "fightin' mad" like being "wicked pissed."

And nothing sums up being "wicked pissed" like the stories of New England's feuds.

So there.

CHAPTER 1

In the Beginning

ON NOVEMBER 11, 1620, ONE OF HISTORY'S MOST FAMOUS SHIPS lay at anchor off of what is now Provincetown at the outermost tip of Cape Cod. Onboard, the Pilgrims (the adult, *male* Pilgrims, that is) gathered below deck to sign the Mayflower Compact. The document was meant to lay out the settlers' collective concerns, allow for majority rule, and help ensure order and survival in establishing a new, permanent settlement.

It may have been the last act of amity in the New World.

Onshore, members of the area's native Wampanoag tribe must have surely had different thoughts as they regarded the strange sailing ship suddenly sitting in their midst. Unlike the Pilgrims' Compact, no document exists of the natives' first reactions and concerns. But we're free to speculate. The late, legendary folksinger Pete Seeger did. He imagined Chief Massasoit, gazing anxiously out at the *Mayflower*, observing ruefully, "Well, there goes the neighborhood."

And indeed, there it went.

The point is not that cooperation didn't exist or happen between the European newcomers and the natives they encountered. It did. (Though it usually involved native helping newcomer.) Indeed, one of the most enduring elements of the Pilgrims' narrative is that of bonding with their new neighbors. What American school-child isn't familiar with textbook images that depict "Thanksgiving" scenes of Pilgrims and natives enjoying a bountiful, outdoor meal together beneath the hanging autumn leaves and harvest sky?

Touching. And what a difference of perspective ever since.

In Massachusetts today, tourists visit Plymouth Harbor to board a replica of the *Mayflower II*, and to take pictures of the golf-cart-sized Plymouth Rock nearby. (An actual rock, yes, but one that authentically connects to the Pilgrims about as much as an actual golf cart.) These days, on Thanksgiving Day itself, at that same spot, New England's Native Americans gather for a National Day of Mourning. Whatever amicable, autumnal breaking of bread did or didn't occur in Plymouth nearly four hundred years ago, it's been bad blood ever since between America's natives and its new-comers. Call it the nation's original feud. Except in this case, only one side—Native Americans—has reason to feel wronged. Perhaps (along with slavery), it's more like America's original sin.

THE SHOT HEARD 'ROUND THE WORLD: STILL RICOCHETING

The same schoolchildren who can picture that "First Thanksgiv-ing" can also recite one of poet Henry Wadsworth Longfellow's most famous lines: "Listen my children and you shall hear, of the midnight ride of Paul Revere." (Which, like the popular Plym-outh narrative, is long on uplifting sentiment, shorter on historical accuracy.) What's fact is that, on the night of April 18, 1775, Paul

Battle of Lexington/Doolittle Plate
THE LEXINGTON HISTORICAL SOCIETY

Revere rode west of Boston, warning residents that British regulars were marching toward the towns of Concord and Lexington, there to seize rebel arms, as well as two of the patriots' principal leaders, John Hancock and Samuel Adams.

What's also undisputed fact is that, just before daylight, en route to Concord, British regulars reached the town of Lexington, about fifteen miles from Boston. What exactly happened after their arrival there, and who played what role in how the rest of the day's fateful events unfolded, is still very much in dispute, and will never be definitively concluded. In fact, almost 250 years later, it remains a point of bitter contention to this very day. Not between the British and the Americans. Between Concord and Lexington.

"There is a certain belief that one side is more right than the other," says Richard Kollen, an amiable Lexington teacher and

Buckman Tavern, Lexington, MA
THE LEXINGTON HISTORICAL SOCIETY

historian who's researched and written extensively on the events of April 19, 1775.

"Still?" I wonder.

"Sure, absolutely."

Hard to believe. Kollen and I are standing outside Lexington's three-hundred-year-old (and recently renovated) Buckman Tavern, just across from the famous Battle Green. Next to us, on busy Massachusetts Avenue, modern cars and trucks streak by. An airplane flies overhead; a power gas mower drones nearby.

"C'mon," I chide. "Sides are *still* being taken here, almost 250 years later?"

"Absolutely. It still exists."

There is, of course, much that is known and that's *not* in dispute about America's most fateful and famous April morning. We know, for instance, that Paul Revere did indeed ride heroically before being captured and detained by a British patrol, after which Revere escaped and continued on with his late-night mission. By dawn, he was present at the armed confrontation in Lexington. (Like a revolutionary Zelig, Revere, it sometimes seems, was everywhere.)

The alarm that Revere successfully raised helps account for the fact that Lexington's famed militiamen were already up and mustered long before British troops reached the town's green on their march to Concord. In the chilly pre-dawn, many of Lexington's citizen-soldiers had stepped inside nearby Buckman Tavern, there to warm their musket-chilled hands by the fire and to have a bracing nip of brandy. As it turned out, they had hours to wait. (Today, visitors can stand in the same, small taproom and stare out the window at the Green.)

What's also undisputed is that, upon arriving at the Lexington Green and facing an armed populace ("rabble," to the Redcoats), British major John Pitcairn commanded the town's militiamen to lay down their weapons and to disperse. Lexington captain John Parker had no intention of doing either one. A brave and patient leader (and dying from tuberculosis), he had already delivered to his own men some of the most stirring words in military history: "Don't fire unless fired upon, but if they mean to have a war, let it begin here."

Alas, Parker could not have foreseen that his men might never know if they were fired upon or not.

And neither will we.

At some point in the tense, hair-trigger standoff, a gun went off. It may have been a patriot's, it may have been a Redcoat's, or it may have been a completely accidental firing. Spooked, the British line unloaded a vicious volley. Mere minutes later, it was all over. Amidst a barrage of musket fire and its attendant smoky haze, along with the piercing screams of both soldiers and terrified onlookers alike,

Lexington Green, Capt. Parker's command to his troops, April 19, 1775
PHOTO COURTESY OF CHRONICLE/WCVB-TV

eight patriots lay dead in the center of their town. One of them had staggered, dying, to the steps of his own home, mere yards away. Ten others, wounded, writhed on the Green as their families raced past the British to their aid.

Braced now for battle (and further endearing themselves to the stunned townspeople), the British let out a loud cheer, fell back into formation, struck up the fife and drum, and continued on to Concord, where their day was about to go very downhill, very fast.

By this point, later in the morning, word of the British advance—and the bloodshed in Lexington—had spread like wildfire across eastern and central Massachusetts. When the British reached Concord's North Bridge, they were no longer facing a small knot of determined but overmatched locals. They were now facing hundreds of armed militiamen, still streaming in from surrounding towns, enraged by the deaths of their compatriots earlier that morning.

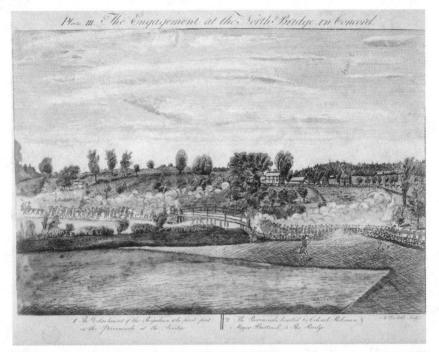

Battle at Concord's Old North Bridge, April 19, 1775
COURTESY CONCORD MUSEUM

A tense standoff ensued, both sides facing off from opposite ends of the wooden bridge. A warning shot came from the British side, then an aimed volley. Two patriots fell dead. In a sense, in that moment, England's ultimate fate was sealed—for the day, for the war. British blood would finally flow.

"Fire, for God's sakes fellow soldiers, fire!" screamed the American's major Buttrick.

Rebel muskets blazed. Three Redcoats died instantly; four officers fell back, wounded. Confused, clearly outnumbered, and suddenly in an entirely untenable situation, the British left their own dead where they lay, and began their forced retreat from Concord. The hunters had become the hunted. By the time the dazed and

Grave of British Soldiers, Old North Bridge
PHOTO COURTESY OF CHRONICLE/WCVB-TV

ragged Redcoats straggled back into Boston at dusk on that long and bloody day, they had lost 273 men. What had been a long-simmering colonial rebellion had burst into an out-in-the-open, full-fledged shooting war for American Independence.

But did it start with the first shots in Lexington, or the first sustained battle in Concord?

"It may not have been clear what would come of this," says Kollen, gazing at the grassy Green where the first shot rang out. "But clearly this was the start of what became the Revolutionary War."

Clearly. Just not in Concord.

For although the Americans would prevail and the British would surrender six years later at Yorktown, it's that war's very first battle that has essentially never ended. Both Lexington and Concord contend that the battle was joined and the war began in *their* respective town. The British were ultimately able to make peace

Minuteman statue and Lexington Green
PHOTO COURTESY OF CHRONICLE/WCVB-TV

with their adversary and put the war behind them. Concord and Lexington have never quite been able to do the same thing.

The basis for the unending feud between the neighboring towns comes down to this: Concord has always considered the "Battle" of Lexington not a battle at all, but a massacre. There was, Concord contends, no real engagement, no real return of British fire. (This last point is quite likely untrue.) Concord has never quibbled with the resolve and heroism of the Lexington militia, nor spared any respect in honoring the tragic deaths of that early April morning. But it was at the North Bridge, they argue (and I do mean argue), that the first real *battle* took place, and the American Revolution actually began. It was Concord, their argument goes, that saw the first, actual, two-sided military engagement of the British, where repeated volleys were exchanged, British lives taken, and the famed "shot heard 'round the world" was, well, first heard.

Old North Bridge, Concord, MA PHOTO COURTESY OF CHRONICLE/WCVB-TV

(In point of fact, that fabled phrase—"the shot heard 'round the world"—wasn't fired off until sixty-two years later when Ralph Waldo Emerson's poem was read in Concord as part of the dedication of a monument at the old North Bridge.)

It didn't take long for things to get downright contentious between Concord and Lexington. Brothers-in-arms soon devolved into brothers-with-a-grudge. And the grudge was nudged seemingly at every subsequent major event marking the events of April 19, 1775. In his well-researched paper, "Lexington and Concord's 19th Century Commemorations of April 19: The Subsequent Battle for Historical Memory," Richard Kollen lists the long litany of charge and countercharge, of engagement and truce . . . long, long after British troops had left American soil.

"Less so now, but certainly at the beginning of and then throughout the nineteenth-century, it was Lexington's identity," says Kollen, referring to the town's sense of itself as the true Birthplace of American Liberty. "And then to have it kind of wrenched from them, by Concord, and then to have Emerson coin the phrase, 'The Shot Heard Round the World,' was fired here (Concord), well, it was a little disjointing."

"And clearly it lingers," I observe.

"Yeah," Kollen offers. "Yes!" he adds for emphasis with a big, wry laugh.

How bitterly ironic that, just like the question of who fired first that day—British or American—the larger question of what each battle represented remains contested to this day. By Americans.

Part of the problem lies in what happened in the immediate aftermath of Lexington. Eager to portray the British as violent aggressors, the Americans blamed the British immediately for having fired first. Intent on getting their version of events back to Britain before General Gage's own report, the Americans deposed the surviving militiamen (all of whom swore they did not fire first), hired a sleek and speedy ship, and in what was essentially history's first major PR war, did succeed in getting their own account of events to London first. Britain may have controlled the seas, but the Americans now controlled the narrative.

"In the original depositions, taken right after the battle, the question that was asked was not, 'Did you stand and fight?,'" Kollen points out. "It was, 'Who fired first?'"

"There is no mention of firing back in Lexington in those depositions," says David Wood, curator of the Concord Museum. "That was deliberate—they wanted it to be 'wounded innocence' at that point, and that was really important. It mattered, what spin you put on this; at that moment, they were all going to hang, and oddly enough, that bit of propaganda worked."

Too well, as it turns out.

Within years of the events, Concord had cleverly begun to use Lexington's own narrative against it.

Wood, an astute and fair man, is standing with me in the small but lovely brick courtyard of the Concord Museum. The Old North Bridge is only about a mile away or so away. Across the street is the home of Louisa May Alcott. Nearby is Author's Ridge, where Alcott, Emerson, Thoreau, and other famed Concordians are buried. Wood, studious and soft-spoken, is steeped in the centuries of this storied town's history. Nevertheless, he seems skeptical of Concord's motives regarding its most momentous day.

"This notion that it was a 'massacre' at Lexington, it's better for the story, the spin. They weren't 'innocent'; many survivors later admitted they had indeed fired back, and then in the 19th century for nasty, spiteful reasons, Concord said, 'But um, you said you were innocent....' It's odd."

Odd, indeed, agrees Lexington's Kollen.

"It used to be the question, 'Where was the first blood spilled?,'" he says. "And then, somehow in the early nineteenth century, at least from Concord, it began to be, 'Where was the first forceable resistance?' So the standard changed."

Each town, Kollen argues, believed they were the more justified claimant to the "Birthplace" title.

Even though, he has written, "the outside world considered the dispute a bit silly."

So did the president of the United States.

A century after the events of April 19, 1775 (and following a hundred years of sniping about who did what that day), Concord and Lexington made plans for centennial observances. At first, there was an effort to make it a joint, unified commemoration. At first. But like a volatile couple that cannot get along for long, the bad blood boiled up once more, the joint efforts failed, and the two towns stalked off and went about making plans separately. (Is it too late for couples counseling?)

Minuteman statue, Lexington, MA
THE LEXINGTON HISTORICAL SOCIETY

"With separate celebrations plans under way, President Grant's attendance became a prize to be won; both sought his exclusive presence," writes Richard Kollen. "Over time, Grant appeared to lose patience with being placed in the awkward position of choosing one town over another."

You think?

American William Diamond's drum, used at Battle of Lexington

Ultimately, a compromise was reached that allowed Grant to visit both towns during the day of April 19, 1875, and return to Boston that evening. But the sniping has never stopped. A century after Grant's visit, on April 19, 1975, President Gerald R. Ford spoke at Concord's North Bridge as part of the nation's Bicentennial celebrations. As I recall, it was a cool, damp morning. But, as a college student, I was nonetheless excited to be standing and listening, mere yards from the U.S. president. I had camped there overnight with friends as part of an alternative "People's Bicentennial" rally. In his official remarks—in his first paragraph, mind you—Ford came down squarely for . . . Concord: *"Two hundred years ago today, American Minutemen raised their muskets at the Old North Bridge . . . the American Revolution had begun."*

And what exactly had begun two hundred years ago earlier that same morning down the road in Lexington? A game of pinochle?

For his part, Wood suggests an entirely different and not undiplomatic approach to diffusing the lingering feud.

"I blame Lafayette." He smiles.

In truth, when Washington's favorite Revolutionary War hero visited the two towns in 1825, "he was a superstar, people would faint, it was as if Washington had come back to life," says Wood. "In Concord and Lexington, it was all about who gets to be on the dais with Lafayette, who gets to be close to Lafayette, so this bickering starts."

And never goes away.

As I was writing this very chapter, Concord and Lexington were at it again. In an indirect way. Both towns were holding dueling exhibits, as it were. At the Concord Museum, a new exhibit called "The Shot Heard Round the World: April 19, 1775" had gathered various historical artifacts that were used on that day. Not to be outdone, the Lexington Historical Society was hosting a new exhibit at the reopened and restored Buckman Tavern. The headline of a *Boston Globe* story put the competing exhibits in familiarly historical terms: "The Old Tavern Debate: Which Town Fired First? Lexington-Concord Skirmish Renewed."

The Lexington exhibit did strive for a balanced, big-picture viewpoint. Called "The Battle After the Battle," the exhibit focused, seemingly without favorite, on a sort of point-counterpoint of more than two decades of inter-town sniping, from the roots of the

Re-enactment, Battle of Lexington/Patriots Day 2014
THE LEXINGTON HISTORICAL SOCIETY

argument, to a comparison of the battlefield monuments ("Dueling Obelisks").

"The premise is to delve a little more deeply into a very interesting controversy," says Kollen. "And that is the ongoing debate over which town began the revolution."

Extending the debate theme, the Lexington exhibit even ends with a ballot box, giving visitors an opportunity to personally weigh in and vote for the "Birthplace of American Liberty" of their choice.

Following our visit, unofficial returns had Lexington with a large lead of over nine hundred votes. (Of course, that's like asking voters to cast their ballots inside the home of one candidate.)

There is a larger irony, with respect to history, bragging rights, and neighboring towns: Lexington and Concord aren't the only two places in Massachusetts that have a valid claim to make regarding April 19, 1775, and the start of the American Revolution. For instance, if Concord points to itself as being the physical *site* of the first actual battle between the colonists and the British, no town paid a higher *human* price in that battle than Concord's neighbor, Acton, Massachusetts. Richard Kollen points out that because Acton's was the only American company at the North Bridge equipped with bayonets, it took the lead in advancing on the British. And thus, it took the first fire, and the most casualties. The Acton company's leader, Captain Isaac Davis, was the first to die at the bridge that day. Because of this, there are those who feel that Acton should be considered the birthplace of the American Revolution. Seems reasonable. However, as Kollen observes, "This argument only had traction in Acton."

Perhaps a stronger claim could be made by Worcester, Massachusetts, New England's second-largest city. On September 6, 1774—a full eight months before the fateful events in Concord and Lexington—by far the largest, most significant, full-scale rebellion against the British took place on Worcester's Main Street. On that day, 4,662 militiamen from all over central Massachusetts converged on Worcester's courthouse.

"This is the largest protest up until this time," says James Moran of the American Antiquarian Society. "It's most of the adult male population of Worcester County, it takes many of them more than a day to get to the city—and this is at the height of harvest season, when they should be tending to their crops at home—but they are so convinced that their government, the Royal Parliament in London is trying to enslave them, and they aren't going to take it anymore."

The colonists surrounded the courthouse, forcibly turned out the stunned British magistrates inside, then barred the doors and shut the building down. In addition, the magistrates were forced to walk a gauntlet while publicy recanting their allegiance to their king.

On a sunny, early September morning, I am standing with James Moran on the Main Street sidewalk where the original courthouse stood. (The original building was moved and is now a private home a few blocks away.)

"Why," I ask Moran, "hasn't Worcester registered more as a place where the American Revolution might arguably have begun?"

"It's a curious fact, isn't it?" he says. "First of all, this was well-known in the nineteenth century, all the early histories of the revolution call this a glorious day, at one point Worcester schoolchildren had the day off. So we lost it somehow, and I'm not exactly sure how or when we lost it."

The answer may be in the colonists' intent to not only stage a rebellion, but to keep it peaceful. They had made the determination beforehand to lay their weapons down at the outset. No one was killed.

"No one's harmed at all, there was no violence," marvels Moran. "These magistrates are the elite, but their houses aren't ransacked like they were in Boston, it's a totally peaceful opposition—it's like a 60's love-in, only it was the 1770's."

"So, let's face it," I add, "it's peaceful, no one gets hurt, no one gets killed, which is probably why no one knows about it today."

"Pretty much," concedes Moran. "If people had died, this might have been truly what we consider the shot heard 'round the world."

There is one Massachusetts town, however, that played its part in sending militiamen to the North Bridge, but has otherwise never rivaled Concord and Lexington for any special attention stemming from the events of April 19, 1775. It doesn't need to. It retains something that not only perfectly and publicly symbolizes the American Revolution, but that also both Lexington and Concord must surely envy to this day. For while its more famous neighbors continued to skirmish for centuries over legacy, the town of Sudbury quietly walked away with a truly coveted trophy—the single-most prized zip code in America: 01776.

And not a shot was fired.

Name That Hill (Correctly, Please)

On June 7, 2006, the TV game show *Jeopardy* went on the air prepared to do something unusual: allow more than one correct answer to the following question: "British general Gage said of the June 1775 battle here, 'The loss we have sustained is greater than we can bear.'" Had the answer unexpectedly been "What is Breed's Hill?," the contestant would have been correct, even as most viewers would have wondered, where in the world is Breed's Hill? Alas, what would have been a rare moment for *Jeopardy*, and an even rarer instance of correcting a historical inaccuracy on national television, didn't happen. "What is Bunker Hill?" carried the accepted answer, the day, and the history books that students have grown up studying. And generations of Breeds in America have been left wondering how it is that their legacy has been reduced to an alternate answer to a *Jeopardy* question. And, for that matter, how does the Bunker family live with itself, anyway?

Annually, on June 17, Massachusetts celebrates Bunker Hill Day, marking the famous, early battle of the American Revolution that took place on that date in 1775. Problem is, the battle didn't take place on Bunker Hill. It was fought on nearby Breed's Hill. It would be as if the battle of Gettysburg had actually been fought in Harrisburg. One of history's most famous speeches would have been misnamed. And Harrisburg itself? You can only imagine.

Bunker Hill Monument, Boston, MA LIBRARY OF CONGRESS

Actually, Allen G. Breed can sum up exactly how that would feel: "We was robbed."

Breed, a writer for the Associated Press, noted in 2006, "To this day I never cross the Tobin Bridge into Boston without gazing at that 221-foot granite obelisk rising in the distance and thinking, 'That should be the Breed's Hill Monument!'"

Indeed it should be. So why isn't it? The reasons go back to the dark, pre-dawn hours of June 16, 1775.

It had been nearly two months to the day since the events in Concord and Lexington. A British force still occupied Boston, but it was a tense and uneasy standoff with a city that despised it, and a restive and growing Provincial Army that was organizing against it just outside the city. There was a simmering sense that bigger confrontations were inevitable and imminent. That evening, about a thousand provincial soldiers set out from Cambridge to Charlestown under the command of Colonel William Prescott. The plan had been to fortify, under cover of darkness, the strategic heights of 110-foot-high Bunker Hill, making it more difficult for the British to operate easily on several key roadways below. The provincials made it to the top of Bunker Hill. But for some reason, their leaders turned their attention instead to a smaller hill a half-mile away. Seventy-five feet high and to the southeast of Bunker Hill, Breed's Hill was closer to the harbor and British warships, and directly faced some of the British onshore gun emplacements. By moving from Bunker Hill and setting up fortifications on Breed's Hill, Prescott and his officers not only disobeyed their orders, but also turned what would have been a purely defensive position into what author and historian Nathaniel Philbrick describes as "an unmistakable act of defiance," thus ensuring a confrontation with the British army below.

Like the question of who fired first on the Lexington Green, it remains a riddle why Bunker Hill was bypassed for Breed's.

"We will never know exactly why they arrived at this decision," Philbrick writes in his bestselling book, *Bunker Hill*. "Dysfunction came to define a battle that was ultimately named—perhaps appropriately, given its befuddled beginnings—for the wrong hill."

"Battle at Bunker's Hill" LIBRARY OF CONGRESS

In the first light of day, the British did indeed discover what had been built overnight on the heights above them, and they did indeed respond to this act of defiance. The British spent most of the morning of June 17 ferrying and landing troops on the Charlestown peninsula. In the afternoon, they attacked, sending repeated waves of Redcoats up the hill. Only after the Americans ran out of ammunition, and only after they themselves suffering staggering losses, did the British finally overrun the rebels on Breed's Hill. The American dead included the eloquent and charismatic patriot leader Dr. Joseph Warren. For the British, it is no wonder General Gage described their losses as "greater than we can bear." Fully half of the British force—1,054—were either killed or wounded. It was a victory Gage also aptly summed up as "too dearly bought." Indeed it was. In fact, less than a year later, the prize would be relinquished, as British forces evacuated Boston, and left the city for good.

Clearly, the fateful battle on June 17, 1775, was a turning point. What will forever remain less clear is why it ended up being inaccurately named. Some would argue that Bunker Hill was a bigger and better-known topographical landmark. There is the argument that it was also the intended military target. All true, but what's also true and more to the point is that Bunker Hill was, quite simply, not the scene of the battle that day. (The "wrong hill," as Philbrick puts it.) And yet its name has forever clung to the battle that was fought that day. Why? Some historians point persuasively to a letter that Abigail Adams wrote to her husband John (who was in Philadelphia at the Continental Congress) immediately following the battle. On June 17, Abigail Adams had stood on Penn Hill, just south of Boston, in Braintree, with her seven-year-old son (and future president), John Quincy. Mother and son stared across the harbor at a distant hill, transfixed by the rising smoke and the sound of booming British cannons carrying across the water. The next day, Abigail wrote a letter to her husband, informing him both of the battle itself and also of the tragic news that "our dear friend Dr. Warren is no more, but fell gloriously fighting for his country." Proving that truth is indeed often the first casualty of war, she also wrote, "The Battle began upon our entrenchments upon Bunkers Hill." Clearly, the misinformation stuck. Over time, it was repeatedly reinforced by others, including that seven-year-old eye witness. Seventy-one years later (as described by Nathaniel Philbrick in *Bunker Hill*), that scene on that long-ago Saturday was still etched clearly in the memory of John Quincy Adams, who wrote, "I saw with my own eyes those fires, and heard Britannia's thunders in the Battle of Bunker's Hill and witnessed the tears of my mother and mingled with them my own." A hill that wasn't even supposed to figure in the fighting saw a tide-turning battle; the hill that *should* have seen the battle didn't, but got credit for it, anyway. And descendants of Bunkers and Breeds, long dispersed from Charlestown, have felt inextricably linked ever since, just like the two original hills named for their forbearers.

For their part, Breed family members have never stopped trying to right this historical wrong. In the 1930s, they finally succeeded in persuading officials to install a plaque just inside the entrance to the Bunker Hill Monument, informing visitors that the actual battle took place not where they are standing, but on nearby Breed's Hill. Small victory. Succeeding generations of Breeds may be less fired up than their ancestors, but the legacy that binds the family seems as strong as ever.

"I mean, it's not like we talk about it all the time," says Jed Breed. "But, you know, anytime you see mention of Bunker Hill, it's still kind of irritating."

A thirteenth-generation Breed, Jed Breed was born in Boston, and moved to New Jersey as a child. He says he became familiar with "the hill" thing growing up, hearing the stories. Today, the thirty-year-old entrepreneur lives in Cambridge, only a few miles from Bunker Hill. He isn't familiar with the AP's Allen Breed, but assumes he's a relative. "Pretty much all Breeds in the U.S. come from the original Allen Breed from England."

For his part, Allen G. Breed points out that there are places named "Bunker Hill" all across America, from California to, well, Bunker Hill Community College in Charlestown, Massachusetts. "And don't even get me started," he writes, "on the aircraft carrier and guided missile cruiser."

Breeds? Not so much.

"Do an internet phone directory search for businesses with 'Breed's Hill' in their names," Allen Breed continues. "And you get two measly hits—Breed's Hill Insurance in Charlestown and its branch up the road in Salem."

Both Breeds and Bunkers maintain longstanding family associations. But Jed Breed admits there's no real contest there. "The Bunker family association is very strong, very active." He laughs, adding, "Hey, if you had bridges and schools and stuff named after you. . . ."

Not that there haven't been some attempts by Breeds to reach out to Bunkers, if only to probe for some acknowledgment of one family's justifiable grudge. Allen G. Breed recounts an email exchange between him and the Bunker Family Association president, Gil Bunker. While he did go so far as to allow that "history does say strange things," Bunker also wrote, "Sorry, Al, we're not changing the name . . . or giving you the monument."

Not exactly the "I feel your pain" response Breed and his brethren would love to hear.

And all those towns, and bridges, and schools, and ships named "Bunker Hill?" Over the phone, I ask Jed Breed if it rankles most because he believes it's all based on a falsehood.

"Not only that," he snorts, "they all know it, too! That's why it's so irritating."

It is no more likely that the correct hill's name will ever gain common usage than it is we will ever know why exactly those militiamen switched hills in the middle of the night. History, after all, is largely in the telling. And the history that has been told is that of Bunker Hill, not Breed's Hill. And that can't be untold. But I do see a solution, if only to let the two families today more directly vent their collective frustrations. (Well, the Breeds, anyway.) While the Battle of Lexington is faithfully reenacted in painstaking detail every year on April 19, the same is not true in Charlestown on June 17. It should be. And the Breeds can face the Bunkers. No aircraft carriers allowed.

SHAYS REBELLION: CAN YOU HEAR ME NOW, BOSTON?

Massachusetts is not a big state. (Okay, it's bigger than Rhode Island, but so is every other state in America.) Given its modest size then, it's not as if the Bay State has far-flung and natural geographical divides. In fact, in most parts of the state, one can drive north-south, border-to-border in about an hour. (Try that in Texas or California.) East-west, from Boston Harbor to the Berkshire Mountains and the border of New York, is just over two hours. And yet, despite the state's relative coziness, there has long been a gulf of sorts between these two ends of the state. A gulf that the mere distance on a map and a different area code just don't seem to explain.

No question, eastern Massachusetts (along with a lot of Manhattan) loves Lenox and lawn concerts in the twilight at Tanglewood. And why not? Far from the city and the manic pace of metro Boston, life sure seems quieter, calmer, and greener out in the beautiful and bucolic Berkshires. Spend a crisp fall day in Stockbridge, and you get a sense why Norman Rockwell chose to spend his last decades painting there.

So it's certainly not as if those in western Massachusetts feel any envy or would necessarily want to trade places with those to the east. But they do feel a bit neglected out there. The state's movers and shakers and those making policy are not moving and shaking and policy-making out in the lovely little hill towns of Otis, Cheshire, or South Egremont.

"I don't think the people in the Boston end of the state have any clue what goes on out here," says Russ Fox, shaking his head. A genial guy, Fox is first selectman and a native of Southwick, Massachusetts.

"I think they just assume life ends down there."

Oh, sure, the west dutifully sends its representatives (and tax dollars) east to Beacon Hill, and dollars dutifully (if unevenly) flow back to the Berkshires. From Boston, statewide candidates strike out on the Massachusetts Turnpike to make their respectful rounds through the hills, foraging for votes in Florence, North Adams, and Pittsfield. And on every visit, they are sure to hear some variation of the same theme: Boston doesn't pay enough attention to us out here in the western part of the state.

"As with many 'feuds,' the animus is largely in one direction," says Peter Drummey of the Massachusetts Historical Society. "Growing up in these parts, I was largely unaware of the resentment of Boston 'out west' until I lived in the Berkshires for a couple of years and experienced the visceral distrust of eastern Massachusetts and everything associated with it—especially in the legislature—which seems to date back to Daniel Shays."

Those were the days. When grudging resentment and visceral distrust exploded into full-scale, armed insurrection.

The year was 1786. It had been ten years since the signing of the Declaration of Independence in Philadelphia, and five years since British general Charles Cornwallis surrendered to General George Washington at Yorktown, effectively ending the American Revolution. Only three years had passed since the formal signing of a peace treaty between America and Great Britain. Across the thirteen colonies, war-weary citizen-soldiers had straggled back to resume their lives in what was then the newest nation on earth.

Little did some of them know that, within a few short years, they would once again be resisting high taxes, an unresponsive government, and punitive measures made to bring them in line.

Forty miles or so west of Boston, the gentle and sloping Worcester hills mark the topographical transition from the state's flat, coastal east, to central Massachusetts, and the even higher elevations just to the west. Forty miles farther, Hampshire County, with its stony, woodsy, and rolling hills, is no one's image of ideal farmland. But then, Massachusetts isn't Iowa. You work with what you have. And the militiamen who returned to farm these hills did just that, eking out—for most of them—the tough living they could. Indeed, their beloved General George Washington had returned to work his own beloved farm at Virginia's Mount Vernon (or at least to oversee his workers there).

But most of the farmers in central Massachusetts who were either returning to their own small farms or starting new ones had problems that the father of their country didn't have: money problems.

The economy of young, independent America was weak, and soon slipped further into crisis. In some places, like Massachusetts, farmers needed all the help they could get to simply hang in and stay on their own land. They didn't get it. Many were forced into debt. In this they were not unique. But these were men who had only years before put their lives on the line to birth a country that now refused to lighten their load by forgiving some debt or printing more money. To make matters worse, not only did Massachusetts governor James Bowdoin, in an already punishing economy, aggressively go after what farmers and others owed in back taxes, but also the legislature added a new and *additional* tax to help cover the state's share of foreign debt payments. Of the new taxes, no less a leading light of the Revolution than John Adams observed that they were "heavier than the People could bear."

Things got worse. Many farmers lost their land, and were imprisoned over failure to pay what they owed. Appeals to the state government in Boston were ignored. (Sound familiar?) In hill towns like Northampton, Amherst, and Pelham, there was a growing feeling that one form of tyranny had simply been traded for another.

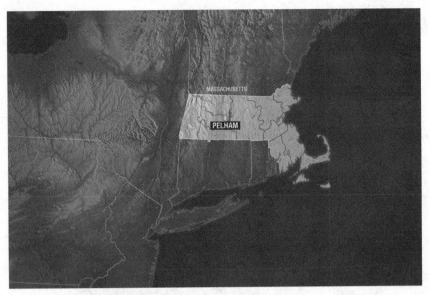

Pelham, Massachusetts GRAPHICS COURTESY OF WCVB-TV

The British had not listened to them, and had imposed new laws and taxes that felt unfair and oppressive. Now the not-quite-as-distant (and duly elected) leaders in Boston, many felt, were doing the exact same thing.

Under similar circumstances, they'd rebelled before. They did again.

Meetings were held, groups were formed, and plans were laid. In the fall of 1786, the rebels forcibly closed several state courts (disrupting legal proceedings), and freed a number of imprisoned debtors. The rebellion grew, and Daniel Shays became the revolt's leader. As such, Shays had perhaps the perfect profile. Born in Hopkinton, Massachusetts, Shays had risen to the rank of captain in the 5th Massachusetts Regiment, had fought at both Bunker Hill and Lexington, and was wounded in battle. He ultimately left the military unpaid, and returned home to farm, where he found himself

Proclamation offering reward for Daniel Shays

summoned to court for nonpayment of taxes, which he could not pay. (Welcome home—thanks for your service.) In an attempt to deal with his debt, Shays even sold off an ornamental sword that had been given to him personally by French general Lafayette. Now,

Shays was leading rural fighters in an armed uprising against the very government he had just fought for.

Today, naturally, there is the vexing question of just how to view this spectacular irony and these tumultuous events. From our perspective, there is some temptation to see the Shays rebels as acting in some of the same spirit as the American Revolution itself. Then again, there's also a strong temptation to see these rebels as America's first anarchists. That's more or less how Governor Bowdoin saw them. So did George Washington, who was persuaded to come out of retirement and crush the very men who had so recently and loyally served under him.

Eventually, inevitably, the crushing came.

Not that the rebels didn't do some damage, make a statement, and draw some blood. They did. But other than closing some courts and emptying the armory in Springfield (Massachusetts), the rebellion ultimately proved no match for a large and well-organized fighting force sent out from Boston (and funded, in large part, by wealthy Boston business interests). The feud with England that the rebels had cut their fighting teeth on was long over, and now, too, was their latter-day rebellion with Boston. Within a year, the rebels were dispersed and hunted down. Most were granted amnesty, but Shays (who fled to Vermont) and seventeen others were convicted of treason and sentenced to death. Of these, only two were ultimately hanged. In 1788, Shays himself was pardoned, and he returned to Massachusetts, where he lived out his life in relative poverty and shame.

It should be noted, however, that the same deep economic unrest that had so roiled the hills of central Massachusetts affected other states as well, like Maine, New Hampshire, and Pennsylvania, where a sense of anger and insurgency, however fleeting, also seethed. But Shays Rebellion became the cautionary tale and the object lesson.

Domestic unrest, once the proud province of patriotism, was now regarded as a mortal and intolerable threat by a state that saw itself as part of a fledgling federal republic. How things change. Men who were once flaming radicals now sounded more like the hated king they once rebelled against. With respect to Shays Rebellion, consider the response of the American Revolution's most famous firebrand and its supreme agitator, Boston's Samuel Adams. Of all people, one might have thought that Adams (like his cousin John) might have at least had some amount of sympathy for the economic duress that the farmers in central Massachusetts were struggling under, and at least some degree of empathy for their sense of rage and frustration toward new and oppressive taxes.

Not so much.

In fact, on hearing about the rioting and the gathering insurgency in the central and western part of the state, Sam Adams went all King George on the new rebels. As Leonard L. Richards recounts in his book, *Shays's Rebellion: The American Revolution's Final Battle*, Adams said, "In monarchies, the crime of treason and rebellion may admit of being pardoned or lightly punished, but the man who dares rebel against the laws of a republic ought to suffer death."

This from the same man who the British Crown was, in fact, hunting down for treason in the build-up to the American Revolution. Not only that, but Adams was wholeheartedly behind the Riot Act, in direct response to Shays Rebellion, which called for the rebels to "forfeit all their lands, tenements, goods and chattels to the Commonwealth . . . and shall be whipped 39 stripes on the naked back, at the public whipping post and suffer imprisonment for a term not exceeding 12 months."

I guess some firebrands never lose their fervor or a sense of simple simpatico with others who share their original ideals. And

Route 202, Pelham, MA PHOTO, DAVID RABINOVITZ

some, like Sam Adams, simply become old, fat, comfortable, and reactionary. No one would argue that a young, emerging American nation could have abided or accepted a full-scale domestic rebellion. Nonetheless, it's striking, and a little sad, to see the viciousness with which a former rebel turned on men who had once rallied to his own call for rebellion.

Personally, I've always thought the best revenge would be for descendants of Daniel Shays to open a tavern in western Massachusetts. They could call it the "Shays Lounge." And ring up sales on Sam Adams beer.

CHAPTER 2

Family Feuds

FAMILY FEUDS ARE AS COMMON AS, WELL, FAMILIES. AND AS OLD as Adam and Eve. According to the Bible, the very first family was riven by a feud. A tragic one, as it is written, involving sibling rivalry between Adam and Eve's two sons, Cain and Abel. As we know, Cain slew Abel, putting a murderous exclamation point on the world's first family feud. (On the plus side, it's possible to take mild comfort in the knowledge that apparently even the very first family had its share of dysfunction.) The book of Genesis tells us that the cause of the brothers' bitter rivalry was anger and jealousy.

What else is new?

Fast forward a few millennia, and some of the same roots of family feuds still show up. And while Cain and Abel may be more about symbol and metaphor than historical reality, the historical record is indeed full of actual, verifiably fierce family feuds. Some have even reached near-biblical proportions. Others have settled in scope for being merely Shakespearean.

The more famous family feuds have generally divided into two basic varieties: *inter*-family (Hatfields vs. McCoys, Breeds vs.

Bunkers), and *intra*-family. In Massachusetts, that latter variety has ensnared some prominent families, leading to some noteworthy and nasty feuds.

Consider, for example, the state's (and one of the nation's) most famous chain of seafood restaurants, Legal Sea Foods. Today's empire of over thirty restaurants in seven states was born in Cambridge's Inman Square more than 110 years ago as a simple grocery store named Legal Cash Market. In 1950, founder Harry Berkowitz's son, George, opened up a fish market and take-out seafood store next-door named Legal Sea Foods. In 1968, the Legal Cash Market closed, and the family opened its first restaurant, Legal Sea Foods. A rough-hewn, almost dive-like place of checkered-topped picnic tables and fish and chips on paper plates, "Legal's," as it became known, also became enormously popular. It was fun and noisy and unique and different. (The full Cambridge "date night" of the period involved dinner at Legal's, an improv show next door at the Proposition—featuring future *Saturday Night Live* stars like Jane Curtin—and an après-theatre stop down the street in Somerville at Steve's ice-cream.) In the late 1970s, the Berkowitzes' focus shifted from the folksy Cambridge side of the Charles River, to the more tony Chestnut Hill on the Boston side, and the family's first full-scale (and upscale) restaurant. By 1980, they had expanded to the city's downtown itself. And the original Inman Square eatery— sitting literally across the street from a firehouse—burned down. Maybe it was a sign of the fiery discord and scorched relationships to come.

In time, like King Lear contemplating the future of his kingdom, an aging George Berkowitz needed to pass along the business to one of his children. And, like the squabbling sisters in *King Lear,* neither of the two oldest sons was willing to share the job. Although George Berkowitz created a new, equal position for his son Mark, the business itself went to Mark's older brother, Roger. Angered, Mark Berkowitz severed ties with his family. He opened a competing restaurant across the street from his family's Chestnut Hill location, but it didn't succeed. Publicly, George Berkowitz has insisted he has no regrets about his decision to leave the business to his son Roger. He's also acknowledged the fact that, as he told a business group in 1994, "I have two grandchildren I almost never see because of it."

Business is business. Companies get dissolved all the time. It's tougher to re-incorporate a family.

The following families would know.

Gunga Din in the Green Mountains

Some famous folks have hailed from the small Green Mountain state of Vermont: inventor John Deere, crooner Rudy Vallee, and two U.S. presidents (Chester Arthur and Calvin Coolidge). Some other non-natives lived there long enough and became famous enough to be forever associated with Vermont, like poet Robert Frost, former governor and presidential candidate Howard Dean (he had the most famous scream since Munch's), and most importantly (I think we can all agree), ice cream icons Ben Cohen and Jerry Greenfield.

Just next door to Brattleboro, Vermont, lies the smaller town of Dummerston. There, you could find yourself driving along a lovely hillside road, with occasional views through the maples and birches across the Connecticut River into New Hampshire. It's Kipling Road, which might naturally make you wonder if it has any connection with the famed British author Rudyard Kipling. Yes it does. In fact, higher on the hill, just past "Just So Lane," you will find the former home of the man who wrote the "Just So Stories." The home Rudyard Kipling built.

Granted, it seems like a most unlikely leap from the British colonial India of palm trees, turbans, and elephants to . . . dairy cows, snow banks, sleigh bells, and sturdy, red New England barns. But it's a leap Kipling made.

And perhaps regretted.

Certainly other literary icons have made New England home. The illustrious list includes the aforementioned Frost, Emerson, a host of Henrys (Wadsworth Longfellow, Thoreau, James), as well as Emily Dickinson and Louisa May Alcott, to name just a few (and Herman Melville, Mark Twain, Pierre Salinger, John Updike, and John Irving, to name just a few more).

But unlike most of these figures, Rudyard Kipling is not generally associated with New England, never mind Vermont. He is, in fact, associated with another country (Great Britain) and culture entirely. Part of that certainly has to do with the fact that Kipling's time in New England was relatively brief. But it certainly wasn't unproductive. In his four years in Vermont (1892–1896), Kipling wrote some of his most famous works, including the Jungle Books, *Captains Courageous*, and a collection of poems containing such signature works as "Mandalay" and "Gunga Din."

Beyond the productivity and the prolific output, the four years in Vermont were to prove eventful for Kipling in other ways, too. But first, some background.

By the time Kipling moved to Vermont, he was only twenty-six, recently married, but already a bona fide celebrity of sorts. He was internationally famous as a writer, and was sought out by local reporters and photographers wherever he went.

"As a literary figure, he was very much a pop star for the time," says Stuart Murray, author of *Rudyard Kipling in Vermont*.

Kipling photo from Elliot & Fry, 1891 LIBRARY OF CONGRESS

"He was a celebrity before celebrities were known worldwide," says Tom Ragle, a Kipling expert and former president of Vermont's Marlboro College, which houses a significant Kipling collection. "The newspapers followed him wherever he went."

The reporters who trailed him, though, were usually disappointed. Kipling loathed the media (What else is new?), and frequently resorted to the nineteenth-century version of today's Hollywood stars' tricks in ducking and otherwise avoiding the pesky paparazzi—all of which is ironic considering that Kipling began his professional life as a reporter. (It truly takes one to know one, I guess.)

Kipling was born in 1865 in Bombay, India, to British parents. As a young boy, he was sent back to England to be raised and to attend school. At sixteen, he returned to India and began working as a reporter for the *Civil and Military Gazette*, a daily based in Lahore. While he had not been a standout student in England, Kipling nonetheless seemed to have been born to write. And he did, voraciously. Back in India, as a young journalist, he began contributing short stories, had a book of verse published, was transferred to a larger newspaper, and thereafter launched a life of remarkably prolific and beloved work that ranged from travel reportage, to poetry, to short stories, to children's literature, to novels.

Kipling left India in 1889, intent on establishing himself in person in London's literary scene, where he was already well-known. He made his way there via a trip around the globe, crossing the United States from San Francisco to Boston, filing travel commentaries and other pieces all the while. In Elmira, New York, he paid a visit to one of his idols, Samuel Clemens (Mark Twain), who later described Kipling as knowing "more than any person I had met before."

Talk about making a good first impression.

A young Rudyard Kipling, from the Bain Collection

In 1892, in London, Kipling married Carrie Balestier, an American from a well-to-do family with ties to both New York and New England, where the family owned land and an estate outside Brattleboro, Vermont. Kipling had met Carrie through her older brother, Wolcott, who had become a close friend, and with whom he was collaborating on a novel, *The Naulakha*. The marriage between Kipling and Carrie was rather sudden, following Wolcott's equally sudden and unexpected death less than a year earlier.

The newlyweds embarked on a global trip of a honeymoon, stopping first in the United States, where they visited Vermont, and the Balestier home in Brattleboro (and where Kipling met his new brother-in-law, Carrie's other brother, Beatty). Kipling and Carrie then continued their trip west, but on reaching Japan, they learned that their bank had gone under. (Kipling was in no real financial distress; he was already becoming comfortably well-off based on sales of his published writings.) On the plus side, they'd also learned that Carrie was pregnant. They headed back to Vermont, and moved into a small rental cottage owned by a local farmer, John Bliss. Appropriately, the happy, young couple dubbed their little love shack "Bliss Cottage." A bit of bitterly ironic foreshadowing, as it turned out.

Kipling took to his new life in Vermont with almost boyish glee. The rural and mountainous landscape meant neighbors were spread apart, and he could interact with people as much—or, better, as little—as he liked. His new home, he wrote with obvious relish to a friend, was "three miles from anywhere." He had loved life in India, particularly Bombay—as hot and as tropical as Brattleboro could be cold and punishing. Yet even Kipling's first Vermont winter, a snowy one, didn't dampen his newfound enthusiasm for his new northern home. Nor did it dampen or diminish his productivity as a writer. In his closet-sized writing room (where he described the snow as laying "level with the windowsill"), he had begun drafting what would become *The Jungle Book*. On December 29, 1892, (with "three foot of snow" outside, he noted), the couple's first child, Josephine, was born.

Life was good in the Green Mountains.

Kipling made some close friends in the community, and enjoyed riding into Main Street in Brattleboro to collect mail, pick up supplies, and have an occasional drink and some lively conversation in the basement tavern of the imposing Brooks Hotel. Within a year or so, Kipling and Carrie decided that their rustic little cottage, as cute and cozy as it was, simply wasn't big enough. They decided to build a new home. Fortunately, because of the extensive acreage that Carrie's family owned in the area, the couple was able to pick a beautiful ridge-top site on the side of a sloping hill that commanded a far-off view of New Hampshire's Mount Monadnock, a view that Kipling took great comfort in. An architect was hired, and plans were drawn up for what would be the Kiplings' dream house. In a fond nod to Carrie's late, beloved brother, they called it Naulakha, a Hindi word meaning "jewel beyond price."

"And that is how I describe this house," says Kelly Carlin of the the Landmark Trust USA, which owns and administers the home. "It is an amazing property, made with love and incredible talent and intelligence and it feels magical when you are here in this house and have the opportunity to stay here." (Because you can stay at Naulakha; more on that later.)

In building the house, the Kiplings hired their next-door neighbor to be the local contractor. It seemed only fitting, since the land transaction itself had involved part of his property, and they had agreed to allow him certain pasture rights on the land as well. All the more fitting since the neighbor was Carrie's younger brother, Beatty Balestier.

Along with his wife and young daughter, Beatty Balestier lived on a farm that had been given to him by his wealthy grandmother, who lived in a nearby mansion. He was a study in striking contrasts with his own family, not to mention his new brother-in-law. He was as brash and loud and free-wheeling as his sister and late brother were bookish, reserved, and genteel. A man of "good cheer and rough humor," according to Stuart Murray.

He was also a drinker.

On an earlier trip to London to visit Carrie and Wolcott, "Beatty became an embarrassment to his cultivated brother and sister," writes Murray. He was sent home. Nonetheless, the older Balestier siblings worried deeply about their young brother, who they seem to have generally regarded as something of an unpredictable "ne'er do well," in Murray's words. In settling down in Dummerston, close to her voluble younger brother, Carrie's plan was to help keep an eye on him, and to help nudge him toward more responsible behavior. It was a plan that, for his part, Kipling wholeheartedly embraced. But it seems bound to have failed.

Beatty Balestier, at least when sober, seems to have been a gregarious, warm, and well-liked man. Kipling later described how his brother-in-law had picked up Carrie and him up at the Brattleboro train station on their initial trip from New York to Vermont. It was a bitterly cold winter night, and Beatty bundled them up in fur coats for the ride home on his large, horse-drawn sleigh. Kipling seems to have been entranced by the sheer newness, the frozen fairy-tale sense of it all.

As the Kiplings settled into their new surroundings, the brothers-in-law, by all accounts, seem to have gotten along quite well, despite the obvious and dramatic differences in size, personality, temperament, and background. Kipling may have been the very picture of a cultured and perfectly mannered Englishman of the age

Kipling's home, Naulakha, 1905, Brattleboro, VT LIBRARY OF CONGRESS

(and he was), but he was not a snooty stick in the mud. In India, he had become friendly with rank-and-file soldiers, and wrote about them with a level of realism and respect that was unprecedented. It endeared Kipling to such "regular guys" his entire career. One gets the sense the same dynamic was at play with him and Beatty, that Kipling was comfortable with and fond of the activity around the farm, and in helping with construction tasks.

"He and Beatty were together often, and between the two of them at any rate, there seems to have been a very cordial relationship," says Murray. "They were pals."

What's more, Kipling fell in love with Naulakha. And to visit the home today, it's easy to see why. Built in a craftsman-style, it looks at once rustic, yet handsomely and skillfully built, with green wooden shingles that seem to blend into its wooded surroundings.

Hallway, Naulakha today PHOTO, DIANE HEILEMAN

Naulakha PHOTO, DIANE HEILEMAN

Most striking, the house is much longer than it is wide—ninety-feet by twenty-two feet. The interior is full of rich woods, inviting nooks, and expansive windows with long views. Through them, the distant hills of New Hampshire seem like nothing so much as immense, rolling waves on the far-off horizon. Which perfectly suited Kipling's vision.

"He designed it to look like a ship," says Kelly Carlin. "He imagined that he would ride his ship house over the hills of Vermont, having many wonderful journeys."

And so he did. At Naulakha, he installed Vermont's first tennis court, and on the sloping hillside beneath it, it is said that skiing was first introduced to the state as well. In November 1894, Arthur Conan Doyle, author and creator of the fictional detective Sherlock Holmes, came to visit Kipling at Naulakha. On the frost-hardened hillside, the two famous authors hit golf balls, while curious locals looked on. Inside the house, in the open, porch-like room known as the loggia ("the joy of the house," as Kipling called it), Kipling

Naulakha, Kipling's study PHOTO, DIANE HEILEMAN

would gather his family together at night and tell stories to his children.

"His children became very familiar with these stories," Carlin recounts, as we stand in the loggia on a cold and quiet February morning, a light snow falling soundlessly outside. "And eventually it got to the point where they would say to him, 'Oh, daddy, tell it just so.' And so it was in this room that the *Just So Stories* were written for his children."

But outside the tranquil refuge that was the good ship Naulakha lurked increasingly troublesome shoals. Next door, Beatty Balestier's drinking continued to be a demon he couldn't shake. He frequently squandered money left for his use by Carrie and Kipling, and seethed with resentment at the help. Although the new house was now successfully completed, the Kiplings felt more frustrated than ever with Beatty, and more anxious than ever about his welfare.

They relied on him less and less, and delegated more to those they trusted more. Beatty felt marginalized; the friendship between him and Kipling and their families withered into creeping animosity. In 1896, Beatty Balestier petitioned for bankruptcy. In a bit of a "tough love" bid to help, Carrie and Kipling offered to essentially bail Beatty out of debt, providing he agreed to certain conditions, such as relinquishing his farm, and having his daughter live with them. Beatty was insulted and incensed. In his book about this period of time, Stuart Murray makes clear that the long-simmering mutual resentment between Carrie and her younger brother was reaching a dangerous pass. Kipling was caught in the middle. Until he unwittingly provided the flash point.

In the basement tavern of Brattleboro's Brooks House Hotel, while sharing a private drink with an acquaintance, Kipling was pressed about the rumor that he had been helping his brother-in-law stay afloat financially. Perhaps momentarily abandoning his unerring sense of tact and discretion, Kipling conceded the point. Undoubtedly, he felt he was speaking in confidence. He may have felt that the rumor, as Stuart Murray describes it, was "an open secret anyway." He may simply been venting some frustration. At any rate, Kipling's words ultimately got back to Beatty, who felt publicly slandered and humiliated. Not long afterward, in the late afternoon of May 6, 1896, Kipling was headed into town on his bicycle, riding down the long, sloping road below Naulahka. Suddenly, amid a clatter of horse hooves, Beatty appeared alongside, where he angrily confronted his brother-in-law. "Trembling with fury," as Murray describes it, Beatty warned Kipling to retract "the goddamn lies you told about me . . . and if you don't do it, I will kill you!" From his detailed description of the scene (based on subsequent court transcripts), Murray leaves little question that Kipling, while not backing down under threat, nonetheless came away from the confrontation with little doubt that Beatty might, especially if drunk, come after him again with malicious intent. Kipling decided to go to the sheriff and file charges against Beatty.

There was now no turning back from the events that would rapidly overtake both men. What had been a long-simmering, painful but private family feud now erupted publicly. Beatty Balestier was arrested for assault. Kipling offered to pay his bail. Beatty refused, and was jailed. Down, but no dummy, Beatty contacted newspapers. Soon, wagonloads of reporters were crisscrossing Brattleboro, as well as the Kipling and Balestier properties. In Boston, New York, and around the world, it was a huge story.

For the consummately, obsessively private Kipling, events were mushrooming into a dreaded nightmare-come-true. And it got worse. As the pre-trial hearings began, Kipling was forced to testify at length in open court. Gleefully seizing on the celebrity factor, newspapers from Boston to Bombay provided blanket coverage. In its morning edition of May 13, 1896, the *Boston Daily Globe* headlined an artist's courtroom rendering, "Kipling in Farce Comedy." Underneath the drawing of Kipling testifying, the caption read, "Kipling airing family secrets."

With the hearings concluded, the judge ordered Beatty to stand trial in September. Kipling's nightmare would continue. But without him. After some late-spring travels to Canada and Boston (where he did research for his novel, *Captains Courageous*), Kipling returned to Naulahka. He loved his home as much as ever. But he and Carrie had decided they must leave it, and sacrifice what had become their idyllic life in Vermont's Green Mountains. For Kipling, life there now was untenable.

Stuart Murray describes Kipling's last hours at Naulahka, pacing the terrace, saying resignedly to a family friend, "There are only

Rudyard Kipling, 1899 LIBRARY OF CONGRESS

two places in the world where I want to live—Bombay and Brattle-boro. And I can't live at either."

On September 1, 1896, in Hoboken, New Jersey, the Kipling family sailed for England. Kipling would later make one more trip to New York. He would never return to Vermont, or his beloved Naulakha.

"Oh, I think it was very crushing," says Tom Ragle. "I think they would have spent the rest of their lives there."

They didn't. But the beloved home that Kipling so cherished is still there. And if you find yourself driving on Kipling Road, you can see it up on the hill, beckoning between the tall stand of trees by the side of the road. The fact that it looks much like it did when Kipling left it over a century ago is by design, not default. When Landmark Trust USA took ownership of the property, it had been abandoned for almost fifty years; the foundation had collapsed, and there was a family of raccoons living in the house. In acquiring famous properties around the world, Landmark Trust avoids turning them into "house museums," in favor of creating "living ones," where visitors can not only experience a famous person's home in every respect, not only touch things, but also stay overnight.

"If Kipling were here today, he would recognize his house," says Carlin. "It looks very, very much like it did when he lived here in the 1890s."

Indeed, there is Kipling's bed, his bathtub, and the kitchen where he made himself a cup of tea. While I've never stayed overnight at Naulakha, I can say that it is a thrill to take a seat in Kipling's book-lined study, at the very desk—wooden and sturdy—where he wrote. But while this experience is both unique and delightful, it also amounts to an elephant-sized irony. The home's original owner was zealously protective of his and his family's privacy. In general, visitors to Naulakha were limited to close friends and family. Now, for a three-night minimum, you can re-heat a pizza in Kipling's kitchen, soak in his tub, and sleep in his bed.

Even jewels beyond price have their price.

A Super(market)-Sized Feud

Most family feuds initially involve two or three people directly. Often, such feuds expand, though, metastasizing like a cancer, ultimately drawing in and involving more people (even those who long swore, "I'm not getting involved in this"). How big can a family feud get? Consider Massachusetts's most famous one. At its height, it involved tens of thousands of people, of which only a tiny fraction were actually related.

By now, the Market Basket supermarket feud is the stuff of both business and law school case study, as well as Massachusetts legal lore. It made national news, and drew international commentary on the subject of labor relations and corporate dynamics. But at its core, it was a family feud, plain and simple. (Well, plain, anyway.) It was also fascinating, long-running, real-life theater, with all the elements of classic Greek drama—including, in this case, actual Greeks.

The curtain rises in 1916, in the mill city of Lowell, Massachusetts, where Greek immigrants Athanasios ("Arthur") and Efrosini Demoulas opened a small grocery store. The cozy "mom and pop" store specialized in fresh lamb, but in time, the Demoulas operation would diversify and grow, leaving its humble origins far, far behind.

Arthur and Efrosini worked hard in their little store for decades, establishing a solid reputation and a loyal customer base. In 1954, they retired, and sold the store for $15,000 to two of their six children, sons Telemachus ("Mike") and George. The bright, energetic, first-generation American sons had big ideas for the little Demoulas grocery store. Nothing if not tireless and dogged, the brothers opened fifteen new grocery stores within the next fifteen years. The Demoulas supermarket chain was launched.

In 1971, the Demoulas family's happy, feel-good First Act transitioned to Act II, and tragedy intruded.

In Greece, no less.

On a family vacation, George Demoulas died suddenly of a heart attack. If the events were happening on stage, this was the point where the masked, white-robed Greek chorus would somberly enter, pointing to omens of fearful and fateful tidings. They would caution the leading character against hubris (excessive pride or self-confidence), and of incurring the wrath of the anxious and all-knowing gods. If such an inner voice of warning ever came to surviving brother (and now sole-owner) Telemachus, he seemed, alas, not to have heard it. In Greek mythology, Telemachus, the son of Odysseus, is a main character in Homer's *Odyssey*. Ironically, the name "Telemachus" translates as "far from battle." In his life, Mike Demoulas would be anything but.

The late George Demoulas and his brother Mike had each owned an equal 50 percent share of their growing supermarket empire. The brothers had made an agreement with each other that, following either brother's death, the surviving brother would take care of the other's family, who would inherit their parent's half of the business. When George's family returned from Greece, Telemachus assured his widowed sister-in-law, Evanthea Demoulas, that he would be honoring the agreement he'd made with his brother. George's children (Mike's nieces and nephews) assumed that their father's shares would now be inherited by them. Their uncle, however, had other ideas.

Gradually, by means both aboveboard and likely below as well, Mike Demoulas began to shift most of the shares of his brother's children to his own side of the family. To paraphrase one of my favorite movie lines, "Not cool, Telemachus, not cool." Not surprisingly, as they became aware (by accident, as it turned out) of what was going on, his nieces and nephews were not pleased. In the early 1990s, they filed suit against their uncle Telemachus,

A Market Basket supermarket PHOTO, COURTESY OF WCVB-TV

and in so doing, assured years of steady work for a small army of lawyers.

If a Hollywood movie is ever made of the Demoulas feud, it's safe to say that the scenes surrounding the lawsuit and its lawyers, judges, and private investigators would be the most marketable and Hollywood-friendly elements. After all, that's where most of the story's sex, violence, and cloak-and-dagger craziness happened ("shenanigans," according to one of the plaintiff's attorneys). There were charges of bribery, spying, electronic bugging, marital infidelity, drug abuse, and improper social contact by the judge with one of the lawyers. Two attorneys were eventually disbarred. How nutty was it? The most memorable moment of the entire trial occurred not in the courtroom, but in a courthouse hallway during a recess, where a fist-fight broke out between Telemachus's son, Arthur T., and George's son, Arthur S. At one point, Telemachus Demoulas spent a startling seventeen days on the witness stand. He and his lawyers argued that his nieces and nephews had essentially ceded to him control and oversight of the family's finances. And besides, the defense repeatedly pointed out, George's kids had never expressed any interest or opposition to anything their uncle had done. And so the case oozed along. But amid the slippery muck and the malpractice, the inching wheels of justice did eventually manage to find traction and grind its way to a decision. In 1994, a jury found that Telemachus Demoulas had, in fact, defrauded his brother's family. It found that, since 1971, Telemachus had systematically transferred $800 million to his own side of the family, leaving only 8 percent of the remaining stock to his brother's family. A judge awarded George's family and heirs a controlling 51 percent share of the company. Appeals and countersuits followed. It was truly the Dracula case—it wouldn't die. Ultimately, however, the original verdict stood. Ten years in court. Hundreds of millions of dollars. An extended family, driven by rancor, bitterness, and greed, publicly throwing dirt at each other for a decade. *Massachusetts Lawyers Weekly* describes the legal saga this way: "The *Demoulas Super Markets* case was a monster, a modern-day Hydra: every time one evil head would be severed, two more would sprout in its place."

But here's the funny thing about hydras and evil, severed heads: you still gotta eat.

One of the ironies (some would say marvels) of the never-ending Demoulas legal saga is that, even while so much energy and focus was directed at a courtroom, the family's grocery business was not ignored. Despite the legal tumult and the soap-opera quality that had come to define it, the family's supermarket empire continued to grow and expand. But the feuding wasn't over. Far from it. Like the undercard at a title fight, new and smaller skirmishes bubbled up and broke into the open. Although George's side of the family ostensibly now had controlling interest of the company, such power on paper only translates into actual control if a company's board votes as a controlling block. It didn't.

The judge in the 1994 decision ruled that each side of the Demoulas family could appoint two members of the company's seven-person board of directors; the remaining three board members would be selected by a majority of the shareholders. To George Demoulas's side of the family, what happened going forward must have felt very much like winning the battle but losing the war.

In the decade following the legal saga, George's son, Arthur S. Demoulas, had taken on the leadership role for his side of the family. He would have liked to have taken on leadership of the entire company. But a nasty dispute between him and his sister-in-law prevented that, opening up a new feud within the same side of the family. The sister-in-law, Rafaele Demoulas Evans, contended that Arthur S. had mishandled the trust that controlled her daughter's shares. (Another evil head sprouts!) Unfortunately for Arthur S., his sister-in-law also sat on the company's board. She exacted revenge on her brother-in-law by siding with the block that supported his arch enemy, Telemachus's son, Arthur T. Demoulas. For Arthur S., there was nothing to do but watch helplessly as his cousin assumed control of the family business. There was, perhaps, some small consolation in his knowing how the wider family dynamics worked; feuds were fluid. The screw would turn again.

For his part, Arthur T. Demoulas threw himself with passion and commitment into his new role as company CEO. He also brought a hands-on management style with a penchant for decidedly fresh, creative, and often unorthodox ideas for running a company. And it worked. For the better part of the next fifteen years, Demoulas Super Markets (which later changed its name to Market Basket) became an industry study in success. Arthur T. Demoulas—referred to affectionately by employees as simply "Artie T."—preached an enlightened corporate gospel of workplace togetherness and collective reward for shared goals. Workers responded. It was as if all the mutual coopera-tion and bonhomie that had utterly eluded the extended Demoulas family itself was miraculously harnessed by the patriarch's grandson, and channeled into the workplace he now oversaw. Morale among employees soared and stayed consistently high. Employee turnover was dramatically low. And why wouldn't it be? For starters, Arthur T. paid higher-than-average wages. (Beginning full-timers earned $12 an hour.) In addition, he instituted yearly bonuses and a generous 15 percent company investment from every paycheck into a retire-ment plan. As happy as the company's employees were, its custom-ers responded positively to the progressive business model as well. At stores with dramatically low employee turnover, a first-name familiarity often developed between customers and store associates. Customers routinely expressed remarkable loyalty to Market Basket. For good reason. Prices at the chain generally averaged 10 to over 20 percent lower than their regional competitors. In time, Arthur T. rewarded (and likely retained) that loyalty by rolling out an across-the-board 4 percent discount on all store goods. And yet, despite this generosity, the company continued to prosper. Its empire of supermarkets grew to three states comprising over seventy stores, and employing some twenty thousand people. Profits were robust. In 2013, the company reported $4.6 billion in revenue. According to *Forbes*, Market Basket had become the 127th largest privately owned American company.

But despite the steady growth and success, not everyone was happy. Specifically, a few people named Demoulas. Like a dormant, demon virus, the Demoulas family's chronic condition was about to break out again. Two decades of relative comity had allowed the company to flourish, and the extended family to reap enormous profit. Competitors were left to regard the peculiar Market Basket model with wonder and envy; few companies anywhere enjoyed such a level of both employee and brand loyalty. But that was about to change. Incredibly, the fast-growing company would soon be brought to its knees, and to the very threshold of ruin. But even the company's competitors couldn't have imagined how the near-fatal wound would be inflicted. How else? By one side of the family attacking the other.

There was always a built-in antipathy between Artie T., and his rival/cousin, Artie S. Demoulas, along with those on that side of the family. Increasingly, those members, symbolized and led by Artie S., came to regard Artie T.'s management style itself with deep disagreement. He was too generous, they felt, too close to the employees, and too distant and dismissive of the board. More than anything, they contended, he was simply not focused enough on ensuring a high and dependable level of profit for the shareholders. After all, an across-the-board 4 percent discount on goods, for instance, might make customers happy, but it represented millions of dollars less for shareholders. They felt that the same was true of the too-generous salaries, the yearly bonuses, and the employee pension program. The company is expanding and doing well, they argued—therefore we, the shareholders, deserve and demand a bigger cut of the profits than we're getting. After all, they said, that's why businesses exist—to make money for its shareholders. It's the classic capitalist business model. Their problem was that Artie T. wasn't running Market Basket like most businesses. And to make matters even more confounding for them, it was working.

"Arthur T.'s business model wasn't based on zero-sum thinking," wrote former U.S. secretary of labor Robert Reich in an August 2014 *Boston Globe* article. "He understood that giving everyone a stake in the business would generate gains for everyone, including shareholders."

And it did. Handsomely. Yes, the yearly bonuses paid to Market Basket employees often added up to several months' worth of salary. Yes, Artie T. had been known to extend months of paid leave to cancer-stricken employees. And yes, the company under Artie T. did replenish almost $50 million in lost employee profit shares after the 2008 financial meltdown. (Artie S. and his allies filed a lawsuit in response.) On the other hand, since 2000, over $1 billion in dividends has been paid to Market Basket's shareholders. Clearly, no one was getting stiffed in the boardroom. Nevertheless, that was the narrative from the Artie S. side of the family—that as CEO, Artie T. was ignoring his principal fiduciary responsibility, that his policies took a bite out of shareholder profits. And in 2013, the other side was finally able to bite back. Longtime board member Rafaele Demoulas Evans, who had kept Artie T. in power by voting with him, switched her allegiance to Artie S., giving him and his side enough power and votes to take full control of the board. Which they did. The screw had indeed turned again.

On June 23, 2013, the board officially fired Artie T. and two of his associates. (Within the week, like something out of a full-scale coup, they also sent police to remove the management team at a local country club owned by the company; apparently all Artie T. loyalists—even those whose purview was golf, not groceries—were now suspect.) Days after Artie T.'s firing, seven Market Basket executives quit in protest. It turned out to be the trickle before the flood. By mid-July, employees at several Boston-area Market Basket stores were handing out pamphlets to shoppers, directing them to a new pro–Artie T. website, "We Are Market Basket." The staff at the suburban Tewksbury store officially demanded that Artie T. be reinstated. On July 18, We Are Market Basket held its first public, outdoor rally. Two days later, the Market Basket board of directors confirmed that it fired a number of employees (most of whom were involved in the rally), citing their "harm" to the company. The rallies continued, and grew. Like a wave, the unrest spread through Market Basket's stores, as more and more employees left work to attend rallies or simply stayed out. It had all the feel and trappings of a massive job action. A job action made all the more improbable in that salaried workers were essentially striking on behalf of a multi-millionaire CEO. Go figure.

"This is why this became such a national story," says Nick Buzzell, producer of the 2015 documentary film *We the People: The Market Basket Effect*.

"Here's this private, non-union company, the workers go out, and millions of customers then join the cause," marvels Buzzell. "They weren't arguing about wages or working conditions—they wanted their boss back! And I think at that moment, a lot of people in America suddenly asked themselves—specifically CEOs and business leaders—what did this guy do to get all that support? How do I get that, and what's the special sauce, you know?"

By early August, one couldn't drive by a Market Basket store without seeing a throng of workers sitting on the road edge of the parking lot with "Artie T. Is Our Boss!" signs. Inside the stores themselves, it became grimmer by the week. With staff depleted, deliveries slowed, then all but stopped; shelves in many stores were practically empty. Customers might have been outraged, had they not reacted with astonishing sympathy to the employees' cause. As if honoring picket lines (that technically didn't exist), they essentially boycotted Market Basket and shopped (and paid more) elsewhere. ("Don't Feed the Greed" was a sign that confronted shoppers at many Market Basket stores.) Many attended rallies, too. It was, all in all, a startling and extraordinary spectacle.

"This isn't the age-old labor versus management conflict," observed Reich. "It's labor, management, customers, community,

Picket Line, August, 2014 PHOTO, COURTESY OF WCVB-TV

Workers outside store, August, 2014 PHOTO, COURTESY OF WCVB-TV

and fired CEO versus greedy directors—something rare in the annals of American business."

Perhaps none of this should have come as a complete surprise to Artie S. or the board. After all, the progressive philosophy of Artie

July, 2014: empty shelves during customer boycott PHOTO, COURTESY OF WCVB-TV

T. that so enraged them is precisely what endeared him to his workers and customers. For his part during this period, Artie T. remained
largely muted and out of sight. (And remained muted; he declined
to be interviewed for this book.) He issued a statement asking that
the company reinstate those employees it had fired. Then, at the
end of July, he and his family's side offered to end the dispute by
purchasing the other half of the company from the Artie S. wing
of the Demoulas family. The Market Basket board of directors
announced it would consider that bid, along with competing bids
it said had been received. But the summer stalemate continued. As
did the growing and expanding workers' rallies. In a truly unusual
move (given that it was a private business dispute), the governors of
Massachusetts and New Hampshire weighed in and offered to help
mediate a resolution. As well they might. Over twenty thousand
jobs were on the line. By mid-August, with stores largely empty,
unable to be re-stocked, and deliveries sitting idle and rotting, the
company was hemorrhaging millions of dollars a week. Industry

Market Basket CEO Arthur T. Demoulas addresses workers on his return, August, 2014 PHOTO, COURTESY OF WCVB-TV

analysts warned that the company's value to a buyer would soon plummet, and began speaking in terms of days, not weeks, before the company faced the prospect of outright financial ruin.

Ultimately, one side blinked. On August 27, a deal was reached by which the Market Basket board of directors accepted the terms of sale by Artie T. Demoulas. As I write this, the final details are still being hammered out, but the basics entail a sale of the company to Artie T. for over $1.5 billion. Artie T. will gain full and sole owner-ship of the company, which has been as profitable as it has been divisive for the Demoulas family.

The little grocery store on Dummer Street in Lowell is a distant memory now, eclipsed by nearly three decades of empire building. Forgotten, too, is that the founder's sons got along well, and built up the business by working well together. His grandsons, who came to loathe each other, nearly destroyed it all. For now, the curtain may have finally come down on more than a quarter-century of this relentless family feud. Maybe. But Greek dramas rarely end so tidily. Just ask Odysseus.

("Family Feuds"): The Skinny on a Skinny (and Spiteful) House

Boston's North End is the city's oldest neighborhood. The first house was built there as early as 1630, the year that Boston was officially established, and only ten years after the Pilgrims arrived on the shore just to the south, in Plymouth. The North End has been home to many of Boston's waves of immigrants, from the Irish, to Eastern European Jews. Its more modern history has largely been shaped by Italian-Americans. A dinner at one of dozens of Italian restaurants there followed by a stroll down teeming and narrow Hanover Street and a late-night espresso at the Café Paradiso or a fresh cannoli from Mike's Pastry Shop is a time-honored tradition (as is audacious double and even triple parking in front of said establishments). The North End is a tiny neighborhood (less than one square mile), whose colorful patchwork of winding, narrow streets is lined with equally narrow, brick, multi-family apartment buildings. So it takes some doing to earn the title of "narrowest house" in the North End and, for that matter, all of Boston. But then, the house that (just barely) occupies number 44 Hull Street has little competition. Or little room to do much of anything else inside it, either.

How narrow is Boston's skinniest house? If former NBA player Manute Bol lay down at its widest point (10.4 feet), there would be just over two feet of clearance between him and the wall. At its narrowest interior point, it is only 6.2 feet across. Having stood in that room, I can tell you I felt like Manute Bol, as my fingers grazed opposite walls with my arms outstretched. There is no front entrance. No room for it. One enters the house through a door on a side alleyway. No room for many doors inside the house, either; different rooms are essentially distinguished by different floors. Who would live in such a four-story, walk-in closet?

Jennifer Simonic and Spencer Welton are among the most recent owners. In an interview, Simonic described the logistics at a party in the house.

"When one person has to go to the bathroom, everyone has to move."

Cozy.

The clue to the size of the house, however, lies not in the question, "Who would live in such a house?," but rather in the answer to the question, "Who would *build* such a house?"

The Skinny House, 44 Hull St., Boston, MA PHOTO, TED REINSTEIN

The historic details of the house at 44 Hull Street are somewhat sketchy, but the basics involve two brothers who each inherited land from their father. While one brother was away serving the Union during the American Civil War, the other one built a home for himself on his inherited land, presumably with the intention of precluding his returning brother from building his own home there as well. The returning brother, enraged, had other ideas. Not to be deterred by the tiny footprint left to him, he built his own tiny house, blocking his brother's view of the ocean.

Clearly, spite is an emotion that is not to be trifled with. After all, it built a four-story (very narrow) home in Boston.

CHAPTER 3

First in Flight: On Second Thought . . .

CONSIDER THE LICENSE PLATES OF AMERICAN AUTOMOBILES, AND the colorful variety of state slogans emblazoned on them. They range from the geographical ("Grand Canyon State") and the whimsical ("Land of Enchantment"), to the numerical ("10,000 Lakes") and the ideological ("Live Free or Die"). Only one state, however, contends that another state's slogan is an outright falsehood. In fact, if Connecticut ("Constitution State") had its way, it would officially strip North Carolina ("First in Flight") of its vaunted wings. Actually, that's already happened. In Connecticut, anyway.

If you've somehow missed this interstate dogfight, you're hardly alone. Indeed, when I first heard about Connecticut's long, ongoing quest for truth and justice in the American sky, I was amazed that such a significant story—one that involves legendary figures and places—could have remained so largely under the public's radar. Ever heard of Gustave Whitehead? Until the spring of 2014, I hadn't, either. I should have; the story was out there. People in Bridgeport, Connecticut, grew up with it.

Gustav Weisskopf UYEN THY HO
FOR THE DISCOVERY MUSEUM AND
PLANETARIUM

In 1987, the story was the subject of a report by the late Harry Reasoner on CBS's *60 Minutes*. It then languished again in relative obscurity until 2013, when, responding to new findings, the state of Connecticut finally lined up North Carolina squarely in its sights, pulled the legislative trigger, and squeezed off something extraordinary: a bill officially discrediting the Wright brothers. The Wrights were not first in flight, Connecticut declared, but rather its own "native son," Gustave Whitehead, was. But the remarkable story begins neither in North Carolina nor in Connecticut. Nor was Gustave Whitehead a native of the Nutmeg State. The story begins in Germany.

Born Gustav Weisskopf (he anglicized his name years later) in 1874 in Leutershausen, Bavaria, he was nicknamed "the flyer" as a boy. By all accounts, he was deeply captivated and obsessed early on with all things that flew (which, in the late nineteenth century, entailed birds, kites, and model gliders). By the time he was thirteen, both of Whitehead's parents had died, and he entered an unsettled period of moving about and adventuring. Over the next six years, he trained as a mechanic, crewed on merchant ships, traveled to Brazil, returned to Germany, and finally immigrated to America in 1893. His arrival in the United States seemed to mark a point where Whitehead's latent fascination with flying became more focused and intense. He got jobs building kites and gliders used in advertising. From New York, he moved to the Boston area, where he got a job involving kites at the Blue Hill meteorological station in Milton. In 1896, he was hired by the Boston Aeronautical Society as a mechanic, and did work designing and flying various types of gliders. But the kites and gliders did not nearly contain Whitehead's most overriding, passionate pursuit. His consuming goal was to do something that had never been done: to get aloft and stay aloft, in a powered, controlled, sustained—and manned—flight.

Wright Brothers, 1910 LIBRARY OF CONGRESS

It's tempting to think that Wilbur and Orville Wright struggled along solitarily in their Dayton, Ohio, bicycle shop, traveling occasionally to North Carolina to nurse and perfect their "Wright Flyer," until it finally flew into the salt air above Kitty Hawk and changed the world in 1903. Not quite. First, the Wright brothers had plenty of company in their quest. And second, the world might have quietly changed with less fanfare a full two years before Wilbur and Orville popped the champagne corks in Kitty Hawk.

Far from being alone in their quest to fly, Wilbur and Orville Wright were competing with others who were similarly attempting to be first to build and successfully launch a heavier-than-air machine that would sustain a manned, powered, and controlled flight. In this regard, the time period of 1895–1905 more resembles the space race of the late 1950s and early 1960s—a seething, frenzied, fiercely competitive burst of inventiveness full of trial and (sometimes fatal) error, as each inventor searched and tested frantically for the small but decisive technological edge that would finally, ultimately, prove the elusive solution to "the flying problem." Already, aviation pioneers like Octave Chanute and Otto Lilienthal had made huge strides in their use of increasingly sophisticated gliders. In 1896, the race quickened, as Samuel Pierpont Langley, secretary of the Smithsonian Institution, successfully launched a steam-powered but unpiloted craft in what would be a sustained flight over the Potomac River. Out of the back of their bicycle shop, the Wrights were hard at work on their own designs; by 1900 they had already traveled to Kitty Hawk to test-fly manned gliders. Back in Ohio, their work turned to constructing a manned—and powered—aircraft. Confident in their basic bi-plane design, they focused more and more intently on perfecting the element of pilot control, which they felt would be the breakthrough. They were homing in.

Gustave Whitehead had been racing, too, with the same single-minded zeal for flying that he'd shown since childhood. In 1899, using a charcoal-fired steam engine, he may well have made a manned, if unverified, motorized flight in a Pittsburgh park. The flight was reportedly cut short when he and his assistant (who was injured) flew into the side of a building, prompting police to bar him from further test flights there. By 1900, Whitehead had moved to Bridgeport, Connecticut. Married and with a growing family, he worked whatever odd jobs he could to cobble together enough money to pay for the materials he needed to work on his airplane designs. (He also relied on attracting outside investors in his work; as to the costs of keeping a home and its occupants fed, he seems to have relied heavily on his wife.) Particularly skilled at engine design and construction, Whitehead was keenly focused on making one small enough and light enough to, well, fly. The engine that he settled on in the summer of 1901 may well have done the trick. Running on acetylene, it was an ingenious design, meant to power what would be Whitehead's twenty-first flying machine. And many credible sources, including contemporary eyewitnesses, believe that it did indeed do the trick. Like nothing else anywhere before it.

Whitehead with friends, daughter Rose WWW.GUSTAVE-WHITEHEAD.COM

The date was August 14, 1901—a day when history may well have been made. In the pre-dawn darkness of Fairfield, Connecticut, Gustave Whitehead was revving and warming up the motor on his "Number 21," a monoplane with a peculiar boat-shaped fuselage. The first rays of daylight illuminated the white fabric of the bird-like wings, which had been sewn together by Whitehead's wife. In the early, still quiet of the summer morning, the motor whined and Whitehead rolled along a flat surface—on wheels, just as planes taxi today. Gaining momentum, Whitehead was up, airborne. In minutes, he was over Bridgeport. Flying at a height of about fifty feet, the craft covered nearly a half-mile, before landing safely and, according to a one account, "so lightly that Whitehead was not jarred in the least."

If the above events actually unfolded like that, then on the morning of August 14, 1901, Gustav Albin Weisskopf made the world's first manned, motorized, controlled, and sustained flight in a heavier-than-air machine—a full two years before the Wright brothers would fly a fraction of the same distance.

Did he do it? Many, including eyewitnesses and latter-day researchers, contend passionately that he did. Others are more skeptical. Still others scoff and dismiss Whitehead's claim with equal passion, contending that there is simply no definitive, conclusive proof that the flight ever happened. And to an extent, that's true. There are significant reasons why the Wright brothers and not Gustave Whitehead get credit for being first in flight. At the same time, Connecticut has not picked (and sustained) a fight over Kitty Hawk for more than fifty years for no reason.

Some things we do know. Four days after the alleged 1901 flight, the *Bridgeport Herald* published what it described as an eyewitness report of Whitehead's flying achievement. (It was accompanied by a drawing, but not a photograph, of "Number 21" in flight.) The story was reprinted in newspapers in Boston and Washington.

"It was on page five of the *Sunday Herald*," observes Dr. Thomas D. Crouch, senior aviation curator at the Smithsonian Institution in Washington, DC.

"The other page five stories on the weeks before and after Whitehead were sort of sensational feature stories—hoaxes, comic stories, that sort of thing—things that were not supposed to be taken seriously."

Crouch is, unquestionably, an expert on aviation history. Whether he is personally the most objective observer in this ongoing dispute is a different matter. Like the Wright brothers, Crouch is a native of Dayton, Ohio. Moreover, as a biographer, he is the author of *The Bishop's Boys: A Life of Wilbur and Orville Wright*. In a wide-ranging Skype interview I had with Mr. Crouch in the fall of 2014, he seemed to grudgingly acknowledge Whitehead as an early aviation "experimenter" ("pioneer" seems to be too generous a description for Crouch), but made it clear that he found the claim of any further achievements both outlandish and a bit of an affront to history as well.

"My take is that I don't think the evidence supports the claim that he flew in either the summer of 1901 or early in 1902, and you know, as this discussion has evolved especially over the past two years, I think more and more people have come to recognize that the evidence just isn't there."

Well, not everyone.

"He was a genius, he invented an engine that ran on acetylene, he created wing warp—all those little wires you see, he could change the air flow, independently of each other, to change the altitude and the pitch and roll of the plane—he was way ahead of his time."

I'm standing inside the main lobby of Bridgeport, Connecticut's, Discovery Museum with the city's then-mayor, Bill Finch. Tall, lean, and gregarious, with short, white hair that belies his young middle-age, Finch and I are looking at a replica of Whitehead's "Number 21," suspended from the ceiling. Like Tom Crouch, Finch feels affronted, too. For different reasons. Along with most Bridgeport natives, he grew up with the legend of Gustave Whitehead, their own local hero who flew first, but never got credit for it.

"We don't have history books that say that Lee won at Gettysburg; we have history books that say that Lee was defeated at Gettysburg," Finch says flatly, arms outstretched for emphasis. "You can't have history books with wrong information."

Much of the credit for what Finch and others grew up learning about Whitehead goes to an intrepid woman named Stella Randolph. A lawyer, educator, and journalist, she became intensely

Bridgeport, CT Mayor, Bill Finch PHOTO, COURTESY OF CHRONICLE/WCVB-TV

curious about the Whitehead story after having been given an old newspaper clipping about his 1901 flight. In 1935, eight years after Whitehead's death of a heart attack, Randolph wrote an article about him for *Popular Aviation* magazine. It was expanded into a book and published in 1937 as *The Lost Flights of Gustave Whitehead*. (A second book, *Before the Wrights Flew: The Story of Gustave White-head*, was published in 1966.) The style of *Lost Flights* is straightforward and reportorial. Randolph researched her subject thoroughly, traveling to Pittsburgh and Bridgeport to sift through surviving artifacts, as well as to take legal depositions of dozens of Whitehead witnesses, friends, assistants, and associates. The books led to renewed interest in Whitehead and, later, to an official request from the state of Connecticut for the Smithsonian to formally investigate whether Whitehead had, in fact, flown first. The Smithsonian has repeatedly declined.

After the renewed interest following Rudolph's book, decades passed. The Wright brothers were world-famous, and had secured a prominent and hallowed place in the pantheon of American icons. Having died poor and largely unknown or forgotten outside of a single American city, Gustave Whitehead had seemingly secured nothing so much as a small footnote in the history (some might say trivia) of early aviation. But his story refused to stay buried on history's scrapheap. Some, like Stella Randolph, continued to probe at why there seemed to be such widespread resistance to investigating Whitehead's work from journalists, historians, and major institutions like the Smithsonian. She found a theory, and a formidable ally, in a retired U.S. Air Force major named William J. O'Dwyer. The two collaborated on further research and a book, which was published in 1978, *History by Contract*. In it, they accused the Smithsonian of having entered into a secret contract in 1948 with the Wright brothers' heirs. As part of the heirs' gift of the Wright Flyer to the Smithsonian, the "contract" stipulated that the institution was barred from ever acknowledging that anyone but Wilbur and Orville Wright made history's first powered, controlled, sustained flight. Furthermore, the authors alleged, such an agreement had had the practical effect of chilling and dampening interest and investigation into other possible flights before Kitty Hawk. Strong stuff. O'Dwyer claimed that the Smithsonian initially denied existence of the agreement. With the help of then–U.S. senator Lowell Weicker (R-CT), he was able to obtain and produce a signed copy of the Smithsonian's agreement with the Wright family. (The agreement can be read in its entirety online.)

"Not private, not secret at all," says Tom Crouch, when I ask about the agreement. "In 1948, when the Wright Flyer came to the Smithsonian, Orville Wright had just passed away, and the executors of his estate put in a single little paragraph in the agreement transferring the airplane to the Smithsonian, that if the Smithsonian were to ever claim that somebody else made a powered, sustained, controlled flight before the Wright brothers, the heirs of the Wright brothers could consider asking for the plane back."

"Can you say that the Smithsonian would be prepared to give up perhaps its most famous possession if, in fact, the Wrights were not first in flight?" I asked.

"I've always thought that, gosh, if somebody ever did come forward with really credible evidence that someone flew before the Wright brothers I'd stand up and say so for heaven's sake," Crouch says, his voice rising a bit. "The point is, nobody ever has come forward with credible evidence that holds up."

That may be a matter of interpretation. Especially to some in Connecticut. And Australia.

By the 1980s, the writings and findings of Randolph and O'Dwyer had introduced a new generation to the Whitehead story, including people like Fairfield, Connecticut, native Andy Kosch. Robust, youthful, and still teaching at seventy-five, Kosch admits that, unlike many in Connecticut, he didn't grow up "steeped" in Whitehead lore.

"I didn't know about Whitehead till later in the game."

Ironically, Kosch seems to share some of Whitehead's traits. Growing up, he was fascinated with science, technology, and mechanical tinkering. A self-described "daredevil," Kosch was also an avid sportsman who enjoyed pole-vaulting and scuba-diving. But he was particularly and passionately drawn to aerial activities like skydiving and hang-gliding. As a young teacher, on a whim and curious about news reports he'd read, he went to a lecture on Whitehead by William O'Dwyer. Kosch found himself fascinated by the story of the self-taught, largely self-trained Whitehead, and the "Number 21" airplane he had built and flown only minutes from where Kosch himself had grown up. Following the lecture, he introduced himself to O'Dwyer. While most of those chatting with

Whitehead with his No. 21, Bridgeport, CT, 1901 WWW.GUSTAVE-WHITEHEAD.COM

the author and lecturer were eager to talk about the Smithsonian's "secret agreement," Kosch had something else completely on his mind.

"I can build that airplane," he declared to O'Dwyer.

And in 1985, with help, he did. No original blueprints existed for Whitehead's "Number 21." But a decade earlier, by using photographs of the craft to determine overall dimensions, aeronautical engineers at Connecticut's Sikorsky Aircraft Corporation had recreated blueprints to aid Bill O'Dwyer in his book research. Kosch was able to use them to actually reconstruct the plane itself. He painstakingly gathered the same building materials Whitehead had used, from Calcutta bamboo, to the same type of fastenings, to the exact type of canvas for the fuselage.

"The hardest thing was the engine," says Kosch. "His engine was amazing—using acetylene, he didn't need a boiler and water—it was 75 percent lighter than a steam engine."

On December 29, 1986, a small crowd gathered on the tarmac at the city of Bridgeport's Sikorsky Memorial Airport. Having finished building his working replica Whitehead plane (and spending $5,000 to earn a pilot's license), Kosch was ready to test-fly his recreation. It took little effort.

"It flew so easily, the first time I was taxiing, a little 15-mile-per-hour breeze kicked up and suddenly lifted me into the air, it scared me to death!" Kosch laughs. "It was so steady, nothing difficult about it all."

"What did your experience suggest to you, one way or another," I ask Kosch, "about the credibility of Whitehead's flying achievements?"

"My flight convinced me that there is no way he could not have flown. Period."

Kosch's flight drew national attention, and briefly reignited media interest in the Whitehead saga. *60 Minutes* did its story, sending Reasoner to Washington, North Carolina, Ohio, and Germany to investigate. But by the 1990s, lacking any dramatic, new evidence or a "smoking gun" sort of revelation, there seemed to be no compelling reason to sustain or revisit the "First in Flight" feud. It's safe to say that, had things simply stayed as they were—a century-old pissing match between some die-hard Whitehead believers and a pillar of accepted history as symbolized by the Smithsonian—it's unlikely that the story would have changed in any significant way. But a decade later, the story did change. The feud was revisited in a new and compelling way. And this time, no one in Connecticut needed to say a word.

John Brown would seem to be an unlikely ally in the effort to steer belated "First Flight" credit to Gustave Whitehead. He had no roots or connection of any kind to Connecticut, the Whitehead story, or even America, for that matter. An Australian, Brown is an aviation historian. In 2012, he was in Washington, DC, doing some research for an upcoming story in conjunction with the Smithsonian. Meeting with Tom Crouch, the subject of Gustave Whitehead came up.

"You know he didn't fly, right?" Crouch said coolly to Brown.

Wrong thing to say to someone who's already curious about the story, has a passion for aviation history, and an unflagging zeal for dogged and detailed research.

"I don't like it when people—anyone—try to tell me what to think," Brown shared with me in an email, recalling his 2012 conversation with Crouch. "My first thought was, 'Really? We'll see. I'm going to check.'"

Brown did check. And hasn't stopped checking. Like a man on a mission, Brown began ferreting out every possible lead in order to answer the question, once and for all, of whether Gustave Whitehead had made history in 1901. His hunt took him to Leutershausen, Germany, where he began studiously going through every artifact in the Gustav Weisskopf Museum. In the museum's attic, he found some old photographs from the 1906 Aero Club of America exhibition. What caught his eye were photos within a photo: in a photograph of the exhibit hall, he spotted photos on a wall, one of which seemed to depict what looked like several of Whitehead's airplanes. Enlisting the help of a local police forensics unit, he had the photo significantly enlarged. Grainy, and black and white, Brown was nonetheless convinced that what he was looking at "could be" Whitehead's "Number 21", in flight. Until that moment, it had been accepted that no surviving photographs of the flight existed.

Traveling with his findings to the I.LA. Airshow in Berlin, Brown met with Paul Jackson, editor of *Jane's All the World's*

Aircraft, often referred to as "the Bible" of the aviation industry. It must have been quite a meeting. After grilling Brown and poring over his findings for over an hour, Jackson concluded their meeting by saying, "You've just changed aviation history."

Buoyed by *Jane's* new public position on Whitehead, the state of Connecticut, needless to say, was enormously enthused by Brown's findings. Legislators reached out to Brown for help in formulating a special commemoration of Whitehead's 1901 flight. But this would be no standard, dry, "In Recognition Thereof" type of boilerplate proclamation that governing bodies churn out daily like so many legislative widgets. This bill might as well have called for recognizing that Ringo had written all of the Beatle's songs. Or that an unknown astronaut from Bulgaria had beaten Neil Armstrong to the moon. On June 24, 2013, with full bipartisan support, Connecticut governor Dannel P. Malloy signed a bill that not only recognized Gustave Whitehead as being "First in Flight" but also officially discredited the Wright brothers of that honor.

(The Whitehead bill brought together more than just Democrats and Republicans in Connecticut. It also made instant allies out of two states long divided a bit by the Wright brothers. Ohio, where the Wrights grew up, lived, and worked, has long regarded North Carolina, where the brothers made their early flights, as a bit of a rival claimant on Wright brothers' fame. But there's nothing like a common enemy to bring two sniping states together. So they can, you know, snipe in unison at a third state.)

For his part, while John Brown remains zealous about the need for accuracy in aviation history, he is equally clear and adamant about his position in the ongoing dispute.

"I'm not a 'Whitehead advocate.' I'm a historian," Brown emphasizes to me. "I wouldn't even rule out that someone else flew before *him* . . . but while it's unlikely that someone else preceded

Whitehead, what the release of billions of words of previously inac-
cessible archive material has shown—once again—is that historians
should never make absolute statements."

And yet, the contested title of "First in Flight" would seem to
be about as absolute as it gets.

"Do you have any doubt whatsoever that Gustave Whitehead
is, in fact, 'First in Flight?'" I ask Brown.

"I have no doubt that Whitehead flew in 1901. That's proven to
the highest standards of evidence—clear and convincing."

While detractors have frequently questioned whether or not
Gustave Whitehead was *capable* of doing what he did, that argument has largely quieted. Indeed, even the Smithsonian has belat-
edly acknowledged that Whitehead had received training, and
more than likely possessed the requisite mechanical background
and technical know-how to have potentially built a machine that
could fly. (No great concession, considering that Whitehead did, in
fact, build and sell engines for others around the world both before
and after his own 1901 flight.) But that's as far as the Smithsonian's
Air and Space Museum seems willing to go. For instance, on the
subject of the photograph that John Brown discovered in Germany,
Tom Crouch barely hides his derision.

"I don't think many folks other than Mr. Brown continue to
argue that that photograph does show a Whitehead machine in the
air."

It should be noted that, while the photograph that Brown
uncovered in Germany was blurry, there do exist other, perfectly
clear photos of Gustave Whitehead posed with his No. 21 machine
(including one in which he is cradling his young daughter) while it
rests on the ground.

Besides, Brown doesn't disagree with Crouch on the subject of
the blurred photo.

"I only ever claimed that the photo was too blurred to know for *sure* what it shows," Brown says. "But the fact that there are news reports describing where it was and what it showed suggested that it *could* be the one.

"They [Smithsonian] added that the entire Whitehead case is based on a blurred photo, which it certainly isn't—I don't cite it as part of the Whitehead case."

What Brown does cite with respect to Whitehead are persuasive elements such as direct evidence, legally sworn eye witnesses, contemporary news reports of his powered flights, Whitehead's formal training and extensive experience in engine building, his earlier experience in designing and flying gliders, and the later successful flights of exact replicas of his Number 21 machine.

Still, history is a funny thing. Decades, or even centuries after an event, we are left with names and dates—even the testimony of eye witnesses—but we can no longer have any real sense of the context of the time in which an event happened, and more, how that context shaped the event. Today, "the Wright brothers" are synonymous with "inventors of the airplane." Yet that was not the accepted, universal truth in the immediate wake of their famous flight. As Stella Randolph points out in *The Lost Flights of Gustave Whitehead*, while Whitehead's 1901 flights received little acclaim by contemporary press, the events in Kitty Hawk on December 17, 1903, also failed to make the front or even first pages of some major metropolitan newspapers. As Randolph details, both the *New York Herald* and the *Boston Transcript* gave the Wrights little more space in December 1903 than they had given Whitehead in August 1901. For its part, the Smithsonian itself did not officially credit the Wright brothers as being "First in Flight" until just after World War II, when—as it happens—the "Wright Flyer" was being turned over to its new caretakers: the Smithsonian.

But there is another layer of historical context that has always struck some as significant in the Whitehead versus Wright brothers dispute: their backgrounds. Wilbur and Orville Wright were, in some ways, the grown-up but quintessential all-American boys. Their family's American roots were well-established, their father (a bishop) was an established church figure, and they themselves grew up in the heart of that most heartland of American states, Ohio. Gustave Whitehead was, by contrast, a total outsider in America, a stranger in a strange land. His parents had died when he was a child; he came to America with nothing but a sense of adventure and the pluck of a young man with nothing to lose and a yearning to follow his dreams of flight. He spoke little English and, early on at any rate, seems to have had an uncertain immigration status, a fact that undoubtedly played a part in his keeping as much in the shadows as he could in both his work and his travels in America. (Sound familiar?) Consider the contested question of photographs of the two fateful flights, Whitehead's on August 14, 1901, and the Wrights' on December 17, 1903. The iconic, black and white image of the prone Orville piloting their bi-plane as it skims over the Kitty Hawk sand that afternoon, Wilbur running alongside, has been called the most reproduced photograph in history. Getting the shot was no accident. The Wright brothers had cameras at the ready that day, and various people pre-assigned to use them. Savvy, and confident of their eventual success, the Wrights were also prepared in advance with a detailed plan for getting the news out to their chosen media outlets. By contrast, Whitehead's flight begins in the shadows—literally—before dawn, with few people about, and no known photographer prepared to document it. For Whitehead, as usual, it was about *not* attracting attention.

Ultimately, though, Wilbur and Orville Wright were the ones who got a definitive photograph of their flight, and Gustave

First flight? Dec. 17, 1903, Kitty Hawk, NC LIBRARY OF CONGRESS

Whitehead, even if he *was* first, did not. That's the breaks, one could say. Nothing fair about life. Or First Flight honors, for that matter.

Regarding the context of the time, however, there is something else. It's worth noting that not only was Whitehead an immigrant, but what his nationality was as well. He was German at a time of often virulently anti-immigrant feeling in general, and rising anti-German sentiment specifically. Indeed, within just a decade of the Wrights' flight, America's allies were at war with Germany. Three decades later, when the Smithsonian "settled" the question of "First in Flight" (and received the Wright Flyer), America had just led its allies in defeating Germany a second time. Timing, it would seem, rarely cooperated for Whitehead.

Wright Brothers Memorial, Kill Devil Hills, NC LIBRARY OF CONGRESS

Bridgeport mayor Bill Finch, by all appearances, is a pretty positive kind of guy. But he has strong feelings and minces no words when it comes to the question of social context, fairness, and historical accuracy.

"The real issue is, he was a poor, German immigrant who didn't have a publicity machine behind him like the Wright brothers did. That's not America," Finch says, shaking his head, as we stand on a bright August day, the tarmac warm beneath us at Sikorsky Memorial Airport. "America is about immigration. America is about the little guy making good on his dreams, and that's exactly what Gustave Whitehead did."

In the enduring and ceaseless dispute over "First in Flight," it can be tempting to see it as an overarching, "either/or" (Whitehead/

Wrights) kind of choice, where one party gets all the credit, and the other is left largely discredited. That's not really the case. The Wright brothers deserve rightful credit for pioneering the concept of the modern airplane as we know it. Their adult lives were single-mindedly (some would say obsessively) devoted to achieving the goal of manned, powered flight. Inventive, creative, scientific, and self-taught, they were relentless in pursuit of their shared dream.

And they succeeded. What's more, their work continued, and their refinements resulted in basic and fundamental designs that are still central to flying today.

They just may not have succeeded in doing it *first*.

"We're not trying to erase what the Wright brothers did. They did great things; they are tremendous champions and pioneers of early aviation," stresses Finch. "But they didn't fly first; a poor guy with a dream from Germany flew first."

It's not likely that this feud will ever really end. As I concluded my conversation with the Smithsonian's Tom Crouch, I asked if anything has persuaded, or might ever persuade, him that the Wright brothers were not first. He repeats, with added emphasis, something he has already said.

"Nobody has ever come forward with credible evidence that holds up."

Credible or not, it's unlikely any further, significant, "game-changing" evidence will arise. Things are as they are. On Kill Devil Hill, in North Carolina's Outer Banks, the majestic, granite, sixty-foot Wright Brothers National Memorial soars above the sands. Administered by the National Park Service, it's a major national tourist attraction. Meanwhile, on a gritty, grass-patched traffic island in Bridgeport, Connecticut, sits a squat, circular marble fountain. In its center, at the top of a gleaming aluminum pole, as if taking flight, is an imaginative sculpture of Gustave Whitehead's

"Number 21." It's a hot, hazy August day, perhaps much like the August day a century ago when Whitehead flew. Cars speed past the little memorial, or stop alongside it momentarily at a red light. Few drivers, or any passersby, seem to take any notice. At the fountain's base, the inscription reads simply:

First In Flight
Gustave Whitehead
Bridgeport, Connecticut
Born 1874 Died 1927

In Bridgeport, they know what they know. And as time moves on, that may simply have to do.

("First in Flight"): *Jog vs. Notch*

North Carolina is not the only state that Connecticut has found itself feuding with. Throughout American history, boundary disputes between states have not been uncommon. Most have long been settled. What's unusual is for such a dispute to still be active or drawing attention today. So you might think that in New England, where most of the first states originated over two hundred years ago, such disputes would be rarer still. After all, the region's six states have had plenty of time to settle any differences.

Think again.

In 2001, The U.S. Supreme Court finally settled a longstanding border dispute between New Hampshire and Maine. (How longstanding? Unclear wording in a decree issued in 1740 by King George the Second seems to have been the problem.)

Further south, in 2000, using modern mapping technology, the town of North Stonington, Connecticut, discovered that a small swath of land across the border in Hopkinton, Rhode Island, should actually be considered part of North Stonington. This did not come as welcome news to those in Hopkinton, who, not surprisingly, had no real interest in switching states. Nor was the finding popular elsewhere in Rhode Island; when you're already America's smallest state, you can't be expected to embrace any further downsizing.

In fact, what is it with Connecticut? Lovely state, wonderful people, colorful history, and enough boundary disputes down through the years to fill a book. No joke: It's a big, green tome titled *The Boundary Disputes of Connecticut*. And that's just the really old ones.

But Connecticut's—and New England's—most interesting border dispute may be one that no court is ever likely to hear. Technically, it's been settled for over two hundred years. But it only takes one glance at a map to wonder how it stays settled, frankly.

"Quite a dispute over the years," is how Suffield, Connecticut, first selectman Ed McAnaney puts it.

"I mean, open warfare has not broken out between Suffield and Southwick (Massachusetts), but nevertheless, it's been quite a little bone of contention."

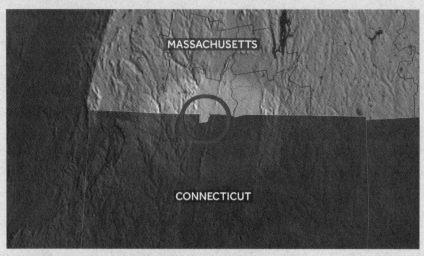

The Southwick Jog GRAPHICS, COURTESY OF CHRONICLE/WCVB-TV

The "little bone of contention" actually represents a rather stunning, little cartographic fail.

It's plain as day on a map. Follow the border west between Massachusetts and Connecticut. At Southwick, for no apparent reason, the border suddenly dips, or jogs, down into Suffield, Connecticut. Then, just as inexplicably, the boundary line lurches left, leaps north, and heads west again, having carved out a roughly two-square-mile patch of Massachusetts into an area that certainly seems like it should still be Connecticut.

"Well, at this particular point, this is still Southwick," says Southwick's first selectman, Russ Fox. "And we will defend our borders."

Fox, an amiable and bespectacled man in his late fifties has a great sense of humor. What he—and Southwick—*doesn't* have is a great case for why Massachusetts should have ended up with this land to begin with. And they know it.

"It's a mistake," acknowledges the Southwick Historic Society's Pat Odiorne, herself perhaps the most genial historian you will ever meet.

"So there's no reason why the boundary line should dip south like that?" I ask.

"No, no."

Blame Woodward & Saffery. What sounds like an upscale furniture design firm was actually the two-man surveying team that, in 1642, was hired to map the Massachusetts border with Connecticut. Confidence in the duo was lacking at the outset; some in Connecticut referred to the two derisively as "the mathematicians," or worse, "the drunken sailors." Which, in part, is understandable. The men were supposed to begin their mapping at the southernmost branch of the Charles River, just southeast of Boston. From there, they were to head due west to the New York border. But fearful of the wide open woods in between, they hit on an alternative plan: they would hop on a ship out of Boston, sail south around Cape Cod, come north up the Connecticut River, then take readings that they expected would match the ones they had taken south of the Charles.

I mean, what could go wrong?

"Well, what happened was, their readings were off," says Odiorne. "So the Massachusetts border ran about seven miles too far south."

Oops.

"I think they just made a mistake; then they stuck with their mistake," says Odiorne with shrug. "Other surveyors came along and said, 'No, no, you have it wrong,' and it went on and on because of other political situations that came up."

That would be situations like the American Revolution.

In 1804, in between "situations" (like the War of 1812), Massachusetts and Connecticut came to an agreement about the border, basically locking in the mistake made by the "Sailin' Surveyors."

To make matters worse, Southwick held on to the area's largest water resource, the Congamond Lakes, which in time served as irrigation for local farms, was home to a huge ice industry in the 1800s, and is still popular today as a year-round recreational attraction.

On a cool, early, April morning, Russ Fox and I stand at the end of a dock looking out at North Congamond Lake. Barely visible, a half mile or so across the water, sits the Suffield, Connecticut, shore.

"All kidding aside, Russ," I say. "You can understand that Connecticut would love to have these lakes back, right?"

"Well, they'll never have it," he says with a smile, looking out at the gray water.

"So, whatever happened with how that Jog came to be, as far as you're concerned . . ."

"It's all over," he finishes my sentence.

For its part, Suffield, Connecticut, has preferred to take the long and resigned view of things.

"Even though it looks funny on the map, I don't think there'll ever be any change," Ed McAnaney says. "We would probably have to go to the U.S. Supreme Court to get that resolved in some sort of way because of a dispute between the states. I don't think there's any stomach for it."

"And if there was?" I ask. "Your counterpart on the other side says you'll never get it back."

McAnaney, a tall, youthful-looking attorney with white hair, grins.

"Well, I'd say, 'We'll see you in court.' But only with a laugh."

("First in Flight"): Foliage Feud

File this interstate feud under "whimsical" rather than "wicked." Its impressive peaks and mountains aside, Vermont is a small and cozy place. The state's entire population (621,000) is smaller than the city of Boston. Until the 1960s, cows outnumbered people. Not surprisingly, Vermonters have traditionally tended to be fairly humble folks, with a natural aversion to pretense or boasting. But there are two things Vermonters are pretty damn proud of just the same, thank you very much: their maple syrup, and their fall foliage. So when the state of Arizona brazenly attacked one of these two pillars of Green Mountain identity, well, things got pretty heated, pretty quickly. You know, for Vermont, anyway.

First, did you even know that Arizona has fall foliage? I didn't. Deserts *and* deciduous trees? I had no idea. But then, I've never spent any time in Arizona in the fall; I've only had the lack of good sense to be there in mid-summer when the temperature was in triple digits. (Yeah, I know—it's *dry* heat.) Apparently, though, by all accounts, son of a gun, Arizona actually has some pretty nice fall foliage. Glowing amber aspens, as it were, to Vermont's flaming maples. The state also publishes a gorgeous, glossy magazine called *Arizona Highways*, full of stunning photos, from canyons and mesas, to mountains and valleys full of . . . well, those glowing, amber aspens. In the fall 2013 issue, the magazine's cover took touting its state's foliage to a new level: "Autumn in Arizona," the cover read. "Why It's Better Here Than It Is in Vermont."

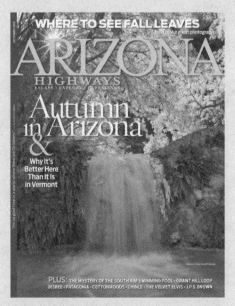

Arizona Highways magazine cover
ARIZONA HIGHWAYS MAGAZINE

Whoa.

It's not likely a single Arizonan took any offense to the cover. The same could not be said in Vermont.

"My jaw just hit the ground!"

Sky Barsch is the associate editor of *Vermont Life*, itself a longtime and well-respected regional magazine. On the phone, she recalls for me the way her day began on August 26, 2013, when she became aware of the infamy unleashed from the west.

"I picked up the magazine, and with no words, just showed it around to everyone in the office. It was just like, how dare they?"

For his part, *Arizona Highway* magazine editor-in-chief Robert Stieve didn't mean to insult or in any way offend the good people of Vermont. Apparently, he has great respect for Vermont and its foliage.

"We set them as the gold standard," Stieve says in an interview.

It's just that his magazine cover seemed designed to devalue Vermont's gold. And reds. And yellows.

"What's great about Arizona is that our fall season starts in early September on the north rim and goes literally until the middle of December in some of the desert regions," adds Stieve. "So, we sort of beat Vermont in quantity."

And effrontery.

"People are so passionate about Vermont foliage," says Barsch. "The gauntlet had been thrown down."

That was a sentiment shared by other Vermonters, especially those whose livelihood depends on those maple trees. People like Burr Morse, a warm, amiable, bearded bear of a man whose Morse Maple farm just outside Montpelier is a sort of shrine to all things maple, especially syrup, which I have had the sublime pleasure of sampling right off his tasting ladle on a cold spring morning.

"Those are fighting words," Morse says of Arizona's magazine cover. (Okay, he was chuckling when he said it.)

Vermont's love affair with its fall foliage, though, is no joke. Far from it. Autumn visitors spend nearly a half-billion dollars annually in Vermont. So Vermont was not prepared to take Arizona's affront without firing back. Well, without doing something, anyway; Vermonters are not

really "fire back" sort of folks. But they are smart, creative, and ingenious. (Where do you think "Yankee ingenuity" comes from?) So rather
than simply take to social media to snipe back, Sky Barsch took to a
more time-honored weapon: parody.

"We should make our own fake cover!" Sky Barsch declared.

So they did. Arizona declares its foliage is better than Vermont's?
Fine. Vermont will declare its own Quechee Gorge is better than the
Grand Canyon. (Which, in truth, even Barsch knows is considerably
more laughable than the whole foliage thing.) The mock-up of the mock
Vermont Life cover read, "Gorges in Vermont & Why Quechee Gorge Is
Better Than the Grand Canyon." To be safe, Barsch ran it by Vermont
governor Peter Shumlin. Good thing, as it turns out, because the gover-
nor wasn't entirely happy with it.

"He tweaked it," Barsch says. "He changed 'better' than the Grand
Canyon, to 'grander' than the Grand Canyon."

Take that, Arizona.

And that's how the mock magazine cover went out on the web.
Everyone had a good laugh, and
in true Vermont fashion, the
velvet hatchet, as it were, was
buried, and calm, positive vibes
returned to the state whose own
license plate should really read,
"Vermont: It's All Good."

"*Arizona Highways* is one of
the best regional magazines out
there," acknowledges Barsch.

See? It's all good.

I do think, however, that
in the end the whole Arizona
versus Vermont thing does
teach us something very valu-
able: Who knew Arizona had fall
foliage?

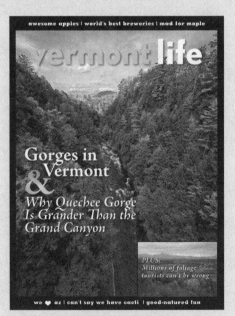

Vermont Life mock cover
VERMONT LIFE MAGAZINE

CHAPTER 4

Food Fights

When it comes to food (never mind haute cuisine), New England will never be compared to regions of France or Italy. I mean, let's face it, its first European settlers were English, historically noted more for stiff, upper lips than adventurous palates. In time, and thanks in part to the region's natives, New Englanders came to take full advantage of what they had to work with, such as a (seemingly) endless bounty of seafood, rolling forests of maple, and low-lying bogs from which to harvest cranberries. How abundant was seafood, for example? In the eighteenth century, lobster in New England was in such surplus that it was considered a "poor man's" food, fed mostly to servants and prisoners. Native Americans used it for fertilizer and fish bait. How times change. Today, from Point Judith to Port Clyde, tourists don silly bibs and pay a premium (some would say extortionate) price for what is now considered—and priced as—a bona fide delicacy. The help is now lucky to get leftovers.

Nowadays, New England still isn't remotely confused with France or Italy, but there are nonetheless some pretty tasty dishes spread across the menus of all six states. Boston's food scene has grown, diversified, and long moved past such musty, old standbys as baked scrod, boiled dinner, and Finnan Haddie. On the other hand, some things endure and remain beloved local traditions for a reason: they're good. Authentic baked beans and fresh corn bread at Durgin Park are still worth the playful insults of the veteran, wisecracking waitresses. To sit at the ancient soapstone raw bar at the Union Oyster House (the nation's oldest restaurant) and gaze over at Daniel Webster's booth (where he lunched daily on plates of oysters and snifters of brandy—then repaired back to the state house), is to have a genuinely quintessential Boston experience. And amid the meatpacking bustle of gritty Newmarket Square, one will find Boston Speed, a simple white truck with a counter window, a few banged-up coolers, and plastic picnic tables spread around it. Alfresco ambience? Not quite. Best hot dog in America? Most definitely. Up the coast in Maine, *Homarus americanus* (very fancy fish bait from the North American Atlantic coast) remains the worldwide gold standard, and stopping at a roadside lobster pound there is something a summer visitor simply has to do at least once. (Twice if you really care about the local economy.) As gold standards go, the same is true for Vermont, which produces the most (and best) maple syrup in America. ("Bien essaye, main non cigarre," as they might say in Quebec, North America's largest producer of maple syrup.) New Hampshire's maple syrup is no slouch, either, and having it slathered on a plate of perfectly golden flapjacks inside the warm coziness of Polly's Pancake Parlor on a crisp, fall morning, as the mist outside rises below the surrounding peaks of Franconia Notch . . . well, tough to have a lousy day after a start like that.

Understandably, there are longstanding and fierce attachments to some of these tried and true New England food icons. And never more so than when a couple of such places compete with one another and their legions of loyalists. Or when a little bad blood mixes in with the marinara. Figuratively, not literally. (I mean, that would be a health issue.)

HEAVY SHELLING ON THE NORTH SHORE

For many visitors to Massachusetts, it often comes as a surprise that the state has more than one cape. To be sure, Cape Cod is the bigger and more famous one. Offshore, it also boasts the storied islands of Martha's Vineyard and Nantucket. And in summer, it boasts a lot of snarled vacation traffic, mini-golf courses, and cluttered roadside signage. Facing west at Cape Cod's tip in Provincetown, it's about forty miles or so across Massachusetts Bay to Cape Ann. More narrow and stubby in shape, compared with Cape Cod's classic "arm-bent-at-the-elbow," Cape Ann's history is every bit as colorful and storied as its more famous counterpart.

Besides Cape Ann's Native American inhabitants, Europeans had already established a seasonal fishing settlement there decades before the *Mayflower's* arrival in 1620. In time, Cape Ann's largest (and only) city, Gloucester, became America's preeminent fishing port. Today, the brutal realities and declining fortunes of the modern fishing industry haven't spared Gloucester any more than Newfoundland or New Orleans. And yet, Cape Ann remains a remarkably resilient place. Against all odds, they still fish. And where the ground fishery founders and keeps trawlers stuck and idled at the dock, Cape Ann's shell fishery still thrives. The lobstermen still head out and tend to their traps all along the shoreline. And Cape Ann's clams continue to be as maple syrup is to Vermont—a delicious calling card, and a point of longtime pride. In seaside towns like Ipswich and Essex, clams are still harvested by the bushel—and so are bragging rights.

Woodman's then . . . WOODMAN'S OF ESSEX

. . . Woodman's today PHOTO, TED REINSTEIN

Bessie Woodman, 1915 WOODMAN'S OF ESSEX

"A lot of history, a lot of tradition—and of course, we invented the fried clam!"

You just don't hear a claim like that every day. But few would begrudge Steve Woodman a bit of deep-fried boasting. Along with his brother and three sisters, he owns Woodman's of Essex, a century-old Cape Ann landmark. In a recent Massachusetts poll of the state's favorite tourist attractions, Woodman's was included along with the legendary likes of Plimoth Plantation, the Freedom Trail, and Fenway Park. Not bad for an old, ramshackle joint that started out as a simple roadside stand selling a variety of things like vegetables, raw clams, and homemade potato chips.

As the story goes, Lawrence Henry "Chubby" Woodman and his young wife, Bessie, were looking for ways to boost business at their new market stand on the slender Essex Causeway. The couple's most popular item wasn't clams (which Chubby dug, but which most customers used for chowder), but "chips" of potatoes that had been cut, soaked, and deep-fried in boiling lard. On a slow and lazy summer morning in 1916, a local jokingly suggested to Chubby that he try frying up a clam—you know, for the hell of it. Chubby obliged, tossing one in the boiling pot, shell and all, leaving the world still waiting for its first fried clam. (According to family lore, the clam exploded.) Next, a shelled but still "naked" clam was fried. This seemed to please no one. It wasn't until the ingenious Bessie covered the naked clam in a corn flour coating before frying it that the "Eureka!" moment finally came. (Offering proof once more that behind every successful man stands a smart woman.) The fried clams, all agreed, were golden-brown, delicious perfection. Chubby and Bessie perfected their creation further, word spread, and soon the struggling little roadside stand was struggling instead with crowds of customers lining up to take out orders of this new taste sensation. Over a hundred years later,

Dining room, Woodman's WOODMAN'S OF ESSEX

Woodman's clambake, 1951 WOODMAN'S OF ESSEX

the scene remains largely the same, in the same location, with the same family. In all, five generations of Chubby's descendants have worked at Woodman's; the sixth generation is still subject to child-labor laws. It's a big extended family, but almost everyone, it seems, stays connected to the place that Chubby launched with a lard-fried clam.

"I started working here with both of my parents before I was thirteen," Steve Woodman says. "I grew up in Essex less than a mile down the street, I live in my grandfather Chubby's old house, all four of my kids worked here, including a visiting high school student from Zimbabwe—his parents returned and he stayed!"

It's still a decidedly casual atmosphere at Woodman's. Wooden booths and big picnic tables. Customers order at a big L-shaped counter; in summer they can sit outside on the edge of the salt marsh. Not that there haven't been any changes over the years. A big part of the business today involves catering, and the huge, custom clambakes that Woodman's has become famous for. And of course, Chubby might faint into the fryer today if he knew how prices have changed. A single lobster roll now nets the equivalent of an entire day's profit back in 1916.

"No question more expensive," Steve Woodman agrees. "Back when I was cooking, late 60s, 70s, we could go through more than sixty gallons of clams in a day—today we might do half that; they're simply more expensive."

I ask Woodman if the family has ever been challenged on the claim of inventing the fried clam.

"People will say, 'Oh, I heard of someone else frying up clams,' but what we've found in our research is that, while others may have certainly tried pan-frying clams, my grandfather was the first to deep-fry clams and sell them. He already had a deep-fryer for his potato chips."

Clams and rings, the Clam Box PHOTO, TED REINSTEIN

The Clam Box, Ipswich, MA PHOTO, TED REINSTEIN

But while Woodman's may have cornered the market on history and tradition when it comes to clams, they are not alone. And on Cape Ann, they don't fry unchallenged.

"Woodman's may have invented them, but I have perfected them!"

There's no problem coaxing Marina Aggelakis out of her shell, as it were. Better known as "Chickie," Aggelakis has owned the Clam Box for twenty-eight years, and runs it today with her son Dimitri. You'll also have no problem finding the place. A few miles off of US 1, along route 133 in Ipswich, it is that rarest of surviving American roadside attractions—an establishment that looks exactly like what it is. (Think of Hollywood's famed Brown Derby restaurant.) In this case, a big, standing, take-out box of clams.

"Yeah, I'd have to say, the building itself is a bit of an attraction," Aggelakis agrees.

Oddly enough, it was built originally in 1935 as an ice cream stand, and meant to look like an ice cream container of the period. It also sold clams. Today, no one comes to the Clam Box for ice cream. Or the kitschy architecture. In fact, it's safe to say that they could rebuild the place into the shape of a shoe box, and the same summer evening crowds would still snake out the door and into the parking lot. Long as they're still frying the same stuff, the same way inside it. For Aggelakis, now approaching her third decade of ownership, that means the same personal approach.

"I'm still here every day, open to close, hands on," she says from her tiny, cramped office above the bustling kitchen just below. "You have to see how things are rotated, if the clams and everything look good, and if they're what you want and what you ordered."

In a busy week in August, they go through 160–170 gallons of clams here. But what may account for the Clam Box's popularity is not any unique twist on the basic recipe, but rather Aggelakis's abiding belief that it's all about the oil when deep-frying clams, and her near obsession with changing it frequently. That means twice a day in peak season. (It also means remarkably non-greasy fried clams.) The "Changing Oil" sign goes up at 2:30 every afternoon, and customers just have to wait.

"It's expensive," says Aggelakis. "We lose almost $200 both times we do it, but it's worth it to me."

And clearly worth it as well to many of the Clam Box's ardent fans. Among them are Jane and Michael Stern, authors of the bible-like Roadfood books. In 2006, writing on their website (Roadfood .com), Michael Stern describes the Clam Box this way: "This the place to eat the best fried clams on the North Shore; and since the North Shore is home of the best fried clams anywhere, these are the best fried clams in the universe."

Here on earth, at any rate, I think that's what's considered a rave review.

And yet, most observers (this one included) would include yet an additional contender on Cape Ann's crowded Clam Highway. Back in Essex, just down the street and literally a seagull's short hop from Woodman's, stands a simple, fading, gray, wood-frame building that hugs the side of the road. If not for the postage-stamp-sized parking lot and the picnic tables on the side, it would be easy to drive too quickly by J. T. Farnham's and miss it entirely. Sometimes, I still do. Better to stop. A true fried-clam aficionado needs to sample Farnham's before passing any judgments on this curious three-way rivalry.

"You know what's funny? I wanted to open it as a deli!"

Terry Cellucci laughs today at the sheer irony of it all. In 1994, with a loan from a local bank, she and her husband Joe bought the place. Neither had any experience running a restaurant. Terry had been a stay-at-home mom working in social services; Joe was

Clams on the creek: J.T. Farnham's, Essex, MA PHOTO, TED REINSTEIN

in high-tech, but his job had become "iffy." Farnham's had been a longtime local seafood joint, but had become "slow and old," according to Terry, and was "running itself into the ground."

But locals made it clear to the new, novice owners that it simply had to remain a clam place. Even if a spiffier and speedier one. So Terry and Joe shelved the notion of a deli, and committed to bringing the place back to life as a clam shack. "Spiffy" didn't happen. In fact, the outside hardly changed. But the food sure did.

"Joe never asks for price on fish or clams, only what's the best you have," says Terry. "One fish vendor finally caught on that even though we're a fry house, we check the quality religiously, and you can't count on hiding bad fish in the fry-o-lator—Joe will return the fish."

Farnham's prefers small belly clams, even though they tend to be more expensive. (Big bellies are easier to shuck, and shuckers get paid by the gallon.) Like Chickie Aggelakis, Terry and Joe Cellucci say the key to clams is keeping them as "dry" as possible.

"We're maniacal about grease!" says Terry. "We also don't batch cook our clams, every clam order is made to order."

While Farnham's has a one-room, cozy, cottage-style dining room, it also sits on a lovely, salt-marsh creek at the edge of the Essex River, which feeds into Ipswich Bay. On a clear summer evening, as the setting sun sparkles on the water and tints the brilliant green marsh grass a deep purple, Farnham's few outdoor picnic tables are snatched up quickly, with cameras and clams sitting side by side.

Like the Clam Box, and its Essex neighbor, Woodman's, Farnham's has its own legion of committed customers. People like John Gilson, a Massachusetts native who I ran into on a quiet, early fall evening at Farnham's, and who doesn't mind making the drive up from the Boston area.

"I go twice a year," says Gilson, who recalls his grandmother's tradition of taking him to Farnham's on his birthday.

"Who's better?" I smile, gesturing down the street without naming anyone.

"Farnham's batter is better than Woodman's," Gilson says.

Over time, such crucial clam questions have been the subject of other inquiries, too. In 2010, the Food Network's *Food Feuds* traveled to Essex to render a verdict on "best fried clams," Farnham's versus Woodman's. Curiously, the Clam Box was excluded. That's akin to barring a leading candidate from an election. But if the Food Network wants to rig a Russian-style result, that's their business. (No one on Cape Ann would limit the question of "best clams" to Essex only.) That said, the Food Network had their winner: Farnham's. In truth, all three places make slightly different but uncommonly delicious fried clams. And ultimately the notion of a three-way feud or "clam wars" on Cape Ann may be overstated to begin with. At least from the perspective of its erstwhile combatants.

"I think that's more about the customers than it is about us," says Steve Woodman. "Anytime any one of us runs out of something, we'll call each other for help, anything from plates to gallons of clams—I'll call Farnham's or Clam Box, and so will they."

"We have a nice rapport with the other guys; Steve Woodman and I talk frequently to compare market prices, etc.," says Chickie Aggelakis.

But the diplomacy is deceptive, and the fried-clam "Kumbaya" stuff only goes so far. I mean, sure they're neighbors, but they're also keen competitors.

I ask Woodman if he's sampled his competition.

"Yes, all the time—gotta see what the others are doing!" he laughs. "I like 'em; Chickie at the Clam Box does a nice job. We just do a better job!"

"Oh, we're all basically on the same page," chides Aggelakis. "But I serve the best clams!"

For her part, Terry Cellucci has never been to the Clam Box, and has only ventured down the street to taste Woodman's once.

"Little greasy."

Clearly, on the contested Clam Highway, pride is not so easy to shuck.

Choosing Sides in New Haven: Pick Your Pie

When my longtime friend Chris Russell tells me something about Connecticut (or baseball), I listen. Chris is not a reporter—which is a pity, because he'd be a terrific one. He has an eye for things most people miss, an uncanny memory for details, and is one of the funniest people I know. Born in Springfield, Massachusetts, he grew up in Connecticut's Fairfield County, in the small town of Monroe. ("Washington camped on the town green," he points out. "Our history hit its high note before 1800.") But over a breakfast of hash and eggs at Johnny's Luncheonette in Newton, Massachusetts, it's pizza we're discussing—and what's up with his native state's unusual affinity for it, anyway?

"Connecticut has three passions," he says, putting down a slice of toast to better tick them off on his fingers. "UConn basketball—both men's and women's—Red Sox/Yankees, and pizza."

Pizza is one of those storied foods for which one can find references dating back nearly a thousand years. (It's unclear when the phrase "No slices!" first appears.) Pizza has its roots, of course, in Italy, and seems to have evolved from the idea of adding ingredients ("toppings" today) such as tomato and olive oil on freshly-baked bread. Most credit its popular origins to Naples, where pizza represented a cheap, filling, and nutritious meal that needed little prep or storage, and could be easily served outside and on-the-go in the city's teeming neighborhoods of working poor. Delicious, simple to make, and adaptable to cultures everywhere, pizza gradually migrated all over the world.

By the late nineteenth century, pizza was being introduced in America by succeeding waves of Italian immigrants. In New York, New Haven, Chicago, Boston, and St. Louis, newly arrived Neapolitans began re-creating the working-class dish of the old country. Yet, curiously, in its native Italy, pizza remained very much a regional food, perhaps even still looked down on a bit by many. (After all, why would cosmopolitan Romans be attracted to a cheap and scrappy dish of the Neapolitan streets?) In the wake of World War II, American GI's who'd been in Italy and had fallen in love with pizza returned to the states, sought out (or started their own) authentic Neapolitan pizzerias, and its popularity soared. Pizza joints, Neapolitan-style or otherwise, began sprouting up across America like (a steaming, stack of larges with extra) mushrooms. Ironically, a reverse cultural migration occurred—as post-war Italians sought to emulate what was "cool" in America, pizza finally became cool throughout all of Italy. The world had been made safe for democracy, and Italy had been made safe for pizza. Even in Rome.

But long before pizza in the United States was as pervasive as it is today—from Chicago's deep dish and California's Kitchen, to Hawaiian-style, wood-fired, Wolfgang Puck, and Papas Gino and John or Pizza Hut—there were genuine Italian immigrants making their new way in a new home called America, making authentic Neapolitan pizza the way they remembered or learned how back in the home of their youth. An energetic young man named Frank Pepe was one of them.

Born in 1893 in the Amalfi-coast town of Maiori, Pepe immigrated to the United States when he was sixteen, and found work in a New Haven, Connecticut, factory. He went back briefly to fight for his native Italy in World War I, where he also married his sweetheart, Filomena, in 1919. The newlyweds returned in 1920 to New Haven to begin laying down permanent roots in America. Like most immigrants of the period, Pepe worked hard at a number of jobs, mostly in the city's Wooster Square neighborhood, which had become the center of Italian life in New Haven. (It still

Frank Pepe, circa 1940 PHOTO, COURTESY OF PEPE'S PIZZA

Frank Pepe's Pizzeria, New Haven, CT PHOTO, TED REINSTEIN

is. The Society of St. Andrew was founded by Amalfi immigrants in 1900; its annual Italian Feast endures as a wonderful, summertime, statewide tradition.) Tireless and a fast learner (although he couldn't write or speak English), Pepe worked for a bread baker, became skilled at it, and left to begin a business delivering his own bread from a cart. In 1925, eager to simplify things, get off the street, and have his own store, he and Filomena settled on the idea of doing something different with their bread. They decided to create instead a simple and familiar product from the region of their youth—pizza. Baking the pies in a coal-fired brick oven, they offered at first just two varieties: what we would today call "plain" (tomato, grated cheese, garlic, and olive oil), and marinara with anchovy. Pepe also rolled out his dough with vigor; his crispy and wafer-thin crusts would in time establish what's become known as "New Haven-style." Staffed almost entirely with relatives and various family members, Frank Pepe Pizzeria Napoletana attracted steady and loyal customers. Word spread about the delicious and authentic pizza, and it became a popular fixture on Wooster Street.

Among Pepe's hard-working crew was his nephew, Salvatore Consiglio. Uncle Frank was clearly an able mentor. In 1938, Consiglio, along with his brother Tony, left the family business in order to establish their own pizzeria. It seemed a bold and brash move for a quiet, tight-knit family. To make things even bolder and brasher, the break-away nephews opened their new pizzeria just two blocks down from Pepe's on Wooster Street. The new place opened as Sally's Apizza ("a-beetz," in the traditional Neapolitan pronunciation). Was it a betrayal? Was it rooted in something worse? Or had Sal Consiglio done nothing more than what his uncle himself had once done—learned his craft well, and left to pursue it independently? Some eighty years later, the truth seems lost in the still-swirling, pungent vapors of the dueling pizza ovens, both of which still bake their respective pies, still a mere two blocks apart.

"You know, over the years, as kids, we heard talk about all kind of things that might have been behind it, " says Sal's son Ricky, 62, a thin man with silvery hair and big, black glasses. "Who knows? My dad and his brother left, started their own place, and we're all still family—to this day, there is no friction on Wooster Street."

That may be true. But to this day, regulars do not amble freely between the two neighboring pizzerias.

You pick your pie. To generations of Connecticut (and regularly returning visitors) pizza lovers, it is very much an either/or proposition. There is no gray area on Wooster Street, only marinara red, or perhaps clam white. Just as you are either Yankees or Red Sox, you are either Sally's or Pepe's. Period.

"I think that's more between the customers, really," Ricky Consiglio says. "We're still family; there is no animosity between the Pepe's and the Consiglios."

"What do you think of their pizza?" I ask him.

"I've never tasted Pepe's pizza."

"In Connecticut, it's like you are a cat or a dog person," says Chris Russell. "It's definitely a criteria. I've known people who've used it for dating someone. Or not."

Ricky Consiglio started working full-time at Sally's when he was twenty-four. It was the 1970s, he'd been living in Colorado, and his dad, Sal, came out to visit. He told him that if he and his brother, Bobby, didn't take over the business, he'd have to close it. The brothers took over, and are still at it.

"I felt a responsibility to carry on the tradition—that was it," Ricky says flatly.

"Ever regret it?" I ask.

"A few times."

Frank Sinatra, as he was wont to sing, had a few regrets, too. (But then again, too few to mention). Being a loyal Sally's fan presumably wasn't one of them. The same goes for the pizzeria's far-flung legion of loyalists. On a midweek night in late summer, they show up early for the five o'clock opening. The line grows quickly. The same is not true of tables turning over inside. No one seems to mind much. (Winter's a different story.) Wouldn't matter if they did. It's one single room inside. Booths of vinyl benches and faded formica tops line the walls, which are covered with framed photos, mostly of Frank Sinatra, posing on various visits there. But your first gaze at this one, warm room will more than likely be from that line on the sidewalk outside. Where you will stand and wait. And wait. Once seated, your wait isn't over. The pies are dutifully baked in the original brick oven in the back. This takes time. This is not rushed. It can easily be two hours from standing outside, to staring at your steaming pie in front of you. At which point, the annoyance of waiting seems to suddenly waft away with the aroma under your nostrils. Takes a special pizza to do that. This is a special pizza. Revelatory, even. Sally's signature charred crust on the bottom seems only to add to the strong and flavorful punch.

It's a busy late August night. Ricky Consiglio is darting about, waving to a friend here, leaning over to shake a familiar hand there. Bobby, three years older and a few inches shorter than his rail-thin brother, is manning his post by the oven, darting back and forth, feeding custom pies into the searing heat.

"That's over 1,000-degrees in there," he says, skillfully guiding a pizza-dough-laden paddle into the glowing, radiant heat that's palpable even ten feet away.

"Your relatives are doing the same thing right now just down the street," I smile. "You guys ever need to borrow anything?"

The line: Sally's Apizza, New Haven, CT PHOTO, TED REINSTEIN

Working the oven on Wooster Street: Bobby Consiglio PHOTO, TED REINSTEIN

"Frank Pepe was helpful to my dad from the start, and always," Bobby says, dabbing his sweating brow with a towel. "If we lost power overnight, or ran out of something, my dad would have me run down the street to borrow something from Uncle Frank."

The first thing you notice about Uncle Frank's is that it is more upscale, shinier, newer. And bigger. No line in front. No need. Two large dining rooms, all wood, chrome, and contemporary lighting. There is nothing rough or worn about it. And the pizza is as arrestingly good as Sally's. On my first visit, I order Pepe's signature white clam pizza, mostly to see what all the fuss has always been about. I see. In the space of a couple of hours or so, I've tasted the two best pizzas in my life. (That includes Italy.) Which is rather extraordinary. (And very filling.) An embarrassment of pizza riches, really, for one, single city neighborhood. No one—New Havenites or anyone else—should be this lucky.

(If Chris Russell and I were dating, we'd have problems. He's Pepe's. I'm Sally's. Somehow our friendship endures. It helps that neither one of us is a Yankees fan.)

"I've had both," Chris allows. "Honestly, it's like splitting the atom. But look, it's not just the pizza; it's the experience. Pepe's always seems to keep order with their line, if there is one, and it moves. When Sally's opens its doors to its restless, salivating masses, there's a sudden mad dash for the handful of tables—sort of like Wooster Street's version of 'musical chairs.'"

Not that Chris is without criticism when it comes to Pepe's. There are the waitresses. And their, um, famed (or infamous) demeanor.

"My dad has always said, 'How can they be so grumpy when they are serving something so glorious?'"

That never kept the Russells away.

"It was like, you got a good report card—let's go to Pepe's! Your girlfriend broke up with you—let's go to Pepe's! Any visitor in town, you'd take them to Pepe's."

There is the matter of Pepe's corporate expansion. While Sally's has remained a one-room affair, Pepe's now boasts no less than six locations in Connecticut, and has more recently opened one in the metro Boston area.

"Granted," Chris says when prodded about this dramatic difference between the two pizzerias, "that does tend to make Pepe's more like the Yankees of the two."

A seventh-inning stretch to address contemporary corporatism aside, Chris needs little prodding to get back to the roots of the rivalry, and his allegiances.

"It might be a myth, but Sally's has always been seen as the usurper, the one who stole the recipe."

Pepe's trademark: white clam pizza PHOTO, TED REINSTEIN

Sally's and Pepe's kids aren't biting. On the myth, or each other.

"Yeah, we took the feud to a new level," exclaims Frank Pepe's oldest grandson, Tony Rosselli, 67. "8000 feet up in Slough Creek, Montana!"

"That's right," chimes in Bobby Consiglio. "Tony and I have been feuding so much we went on a month-long fly-fishing trip."

It goes on like this. I have both men on the phone; they're in the car, having just done some shopping together for fishing gear.

"Hey, we have to get along," Consiglio laughs. "I have no other cousins who can handle a fly rod."

Unlike his cousin, Ricky, Tony Rosselli has tasted his grandfather's competition down the street.

"Sally's pizza is great!" says Rosselli. "Our pizzas are different, but in a way, they're the same. For me, nothing but good memories.

Thin crust at Sally's PHOTO, TED REINSTEIN

Years ago, I was dropping something by there, and Sal's wife, Flo, asked me if I wanted some pizza. Hey, she's an Italian mom—she wanted to feed me!"

Big, mutual laughs from the cousins' end of the phone.

But guys—what about the feud?

"It's the customers, really," says Bobby Consiglio, echoing his younger brother. "When my dad died in 1989, all the Pepe's were right there at the funeral."

"We're bookends on Wooster Street," adds Rosselli. "Best way I can put it."

Bookends. With volumes full of colorful and tasty—if not feuding—family history between them, still sitting prominently, proudly, and pungently on the living shelf that is New Haven's Wooster Street.

Best way I can put it.

("Food Fights"): Pouring It On

In New England, it's enough to simply ask, "Is there a 'Dunkin's around here?" No need to say more. A New Englander knows. True, Starbucks is only one word, not two, but in any event, there's no abbreviating it. No nickname. Nicknames are for friends and family.

After some sixty-five years, few brands are as familiar in New England as Dunkin' Donuts. Founder William Rosenberg opened his first restaurant, Open Kettle, in Quincy, Massachusetts, in 1948. The name was changed (permanently) to Dunkin' Donuts in 1950. People seemed to like the simple concept of fresh-baked donuts and fresh-brewed coffee. Little more than ten years later, there were a hundred stores. Today, the company's ubiquitous orange and pink signs seem as much a part of the New England landscape as birch trees or spoked "B's" (Bruins logo), and one can now find a "Dunkin's" all over the world.

Of course, the same is true of Starbucks. And while New Englanders may want to deny it, Starbucks is even more ubiqitous. Dunkin' Donuts' slogan is, "America Runs on Dunkin'." Not quite. The reality, perhaps a bitter (Styrofoam) cup to swallow in New England, is that the nation seems instead to run on Starbucks. The numbers don't lie; there are over eleven thousand Starbucks in the United States; there are just over seven thousand Dunkin' Donuts. Worldwide, the gap is even bigger: there are over twenty-one thousand Starbucks across the globe. Outside the United States, there are just over three thousand Dunkin' Donuts. Munchkins, unlike macchiatos, apparently have yet to truly conquer the world.

But when it comes to coffee and donuts, the numbers don't tell the whole story. For starters, don't look for a donut at Starbucks. (A bit lowbrow for latte lovers.) And when ordering your coffee size, best to brush up on your Italian ("Venti"). Or is it French ("Grande")? One DD commercial, mocking Starbucks' peculiar menu patois, refers to it as "Fritalian." Want a "small"? That will be a "Tall." Want a medium? That will be a "Grande," which, if I recall my French correctly, means "large." (Starbucks now also offers a "Trenta," which sounds curiously like a small, Soviet-era automobile.) But why get hung up on mere words? It's more

Coffee Clash PHOTO, TED REINSTEIN

about milieu. Which actually is an actual French word, and not a beverage size. Dictionary.com defines *milieu* as "surroundings, especially of a social or cultural nature." And that's really the essence of the Starbucks/Dunkin' divide. It's more about culture than coffee.

Ironically, both companies share certain biographical details. Both began as purely regional brands with a strong, local following (DD in the Northeast, Starbucks in the Northwest) before expanding nationally and internationally. For many years, Dunkin' Donuts was more about its donuts than its coffee. Starbucks was always about high-end (and heavily roasted) coffee. And Dunkin' Donuts hasn't been beyond some silly menu offerings of its own. (A "Dunkaccino" isn't fooling anyone; neither is a "Snack N' Go Chicken Wrap" making anyone forget about donuts.) But ultimately, there remains a more blue-collar ethos associated with Dunkin' Donuts than with Starbucks. These are simply two companies with dramatically different appeals. Personally, I'm a Dunkin' guy; always have been. Sure, I've darkened the door of a Starbucks or two. But as I drive about New England, I pride myself on knowing the exits that lead most quickly to a Dunk.

Maybe it's a regional thing; maybe it's being a creature of habit. Maybe it's the crullers and the butternut donuts. (I think it is, actually.) But the two rival coffee camps remain just that—rivals.

Making the donuts, pouring the coffee, steaming the lattes, and frapping the frappuccinos, locked in an endless and highly caffeinated contest from which neither can claim total victory and unchallenged world domination.

Or can they?

It could be argued that Super Bowl XLIX in Glendale, Arizona, on February 1, 2015, was a showdown between both America's two best football teams and, in a bit of a proxy battle, the home bases—New England and Seattle—of America's two biggest coffee chains. The Patriots defeated the Seahawks, 28–24 (with fully inflated footballs).

Just sayin'.

CHAPTER 5

The Rivalry

Bart (commissioner Giammati, a lifelong Red Sox fan) would look up at me and say, "Can you believe this man is a Yankee fan?" He made it sound like I was a child molester.
— FAY VINCENT, COMMISSIONER OF MAJOR
LEAGUE BASEBALL, 1989–1992
(*RED SOX VS. YANKEES: THE GREAT RIVALRY*,
BY HARVEY FROMMER AND FREDERIC J. FROMMER)

ALL SPORTS HAVE THEIR RIVALRIES. STARTING WITH FOOTBALL. (No, not the Army-Navy, Harvard-Yale variety.)

Soccer. For the rest of the world, *the* international football rivalry is Brazil versus Argentina. Then there are the leagues of professional club teams within many soccer-obsessed countries. In many cases, the word *rivalry* doesn't even begin to describe the level of passion and near-hysteria. People can get killed. And have.

In the United States, things are a bit tamer. Or at least its sports rivalries tend to generate a lower body count (but a higher level of merchandising). Many of America's greatest sports rivalries, particularly in major league baseball, are regional in origin. On the West Coast, the Giants and Dodgers have clubbed each other (literally, in one famous instance) for decades. For a century, the "Route 66 Rivalry"— St. Louis Cardinals versus Chicago Cubs—has been the Midwest's marquee match-up, and one of baseball's most enduring ones.

But it's the Midwest. People may be passionate and partisan, but it's still polite. The fans in St. Louis don't toss batteries from the upper deck onto the visiting Cubs outfielders. In Chicago, there are no prolonged, booming, bleacher-wide chants of "Cards Suck!" (Although I have witnessed nudity and drunkenness at Wrigley.) No, to observe that level of rivalry—and the utter absence of anything approaching polite—you have to be in New York or Boston. The Rivalry. Like Brazil versus Argentina. But for baseball.

"There are so many levels to it—it's like peeling an onion," says Richard Johnson, curator of the New England Sports Museum and co-author (with Glenn Stout) of *Red Sox Century*. "There aren't many rivalries—in anything—where the mythology of it competes with the actual history."

Former New York Yankees pitcher Jim Bouton got his history lesson early. He broke into the big leagues as a rookie in 1962. Older players took delight in schooling the rookies on rudiments of the Rivalry.

"I heard about it in spring training before we even broke camp," says Bouton. "The vets would say, 'Oh, wait till you get to Boston, wait till you get to Fenway.'"

And when he did get to Fenway for the first time?

"The team bus pulled up, 3 p.m. or so for an 8 p.m. game," Bouton recalls. "We walked in toward the visiting locker room, and there's like 250 people in the middle of the afternoon standing there, razzing us, taunting us—like it was a play-off game. And I thought to myself, 'These people are nuts!'"

Jim Bouton, spring training, circa 1962 NATIONAL BASEBALL HALL OF FAME LIBRARY,
COOPERSTOWN, NY

Bill Lee NATIONAL BASEBALL HALL OF FAME LIBRARY, COOPERSTOWN, NY

It was a similar experience for Sox players coming in to New York.

"You felt a lot of anxiety, more on edge going into New York than anywhere else, for sure," says former Red Sox pitcher Bill Lee. "We didn't speak the same language."

True enough. Bouton admits he sometimes heard expressions screamed from the Fenway stands that, as he recalls, "I couldn't even understand!"

Now 76, Bouton is known as much for being an All-Star pitcher (21-7 in 1963) as he is for writing one of the most significant books in sports history, *Ball Four*, a groundbreaking and decidedly irreverent memoir of his decidedly colorful pitching career, from the giddy days of the World Champion Yankees, to the crazy days of the expansion-era Seattle Pilots in 1969. For the past twenty years, Bouton and his wife have lived in the Berkshire hills of Western Massachusetts—in the heart of Red Sox country. It's an ironic fact that Bouton's wife, Paula, has occasionally felt compelled to remind him of.

"One fall day I was raking leaves outside, and I had an old Yankees hat on," laughs Bouton. "And Paula said, 'Not sure you should be wearing that hat, honey—it's hunting season.'"

In truth, it's been hunting season—for both sides—for a long, long time. Few quarries have stalked each other longer, or have known each other better. Indeed, no rivalry in sports more vividly illustrates the old adage, "Familiarity breeds contempt." The Red Sox and the Yankees have been competing against each other for over a hundred years. They have faced each other more than any other two teams. In fact, they have been competing against each other since before there even *were* Red Sox and Yankees.

On May 7, 1903, at Boston's Huntington Avenue Grounds (now the site of Northeastern University), the Pilgrims faced the Highlanders. In time, the Pilgrims would become the Red Sox; the Highlanders were the future Yankees. But this was the first game between the two franchises as we essentially know them today. In a harbinger of the irony that would always surround the two teams, Boston defeated New York that day, 6-2. A fortune teller with a taste for cynicism might have said to the Sox afterward, "Nice game—but don't get used to it."

More than two thousand games have followed that first one. As of winter 2015, the Yankees hold the clear advantage in overall wins (1,152) and World Championships (27). And while there are no official statistics for it, New York also leads, hands-down, in the unofficial category of crucial-games-won-that-resulted-in-Boston-hearts-broken-pride-punctured-and-dreams-busted. (Sometimes brutally.) But the official record, long and colorful as it may be, tells a mere sliver of the story. Nor does it convey the deep and complex human strands that have woven their way through it. Because the Sox-Yankees rivalry is more than a story about two teams. It is also very much the tale of two cities.

First, full disclosure: I was born in Boston and grew up in Winthrop, Massachusetts, a small peninsula of a town jutting out into the northeastern edge of Boston Harbor. While my all-time favorite baseball team is the long-gone Brooklyn Dodgers (I've also lived in Brooklyn and Manhattan), I do subscribe to the rule that, ultimately, you have to be "true to your school." I saw my first Sox game at six, and like legions of Boston fans, will never forget the first breathtaking moment of walking up the runway from under the dark, dank grandstands, being almost blinded by the towering lights above the left-field wall (the Monster), and stopping mid-step, eyes wide, to fully take in that first, lush, full-green flush of Fenway Park.

New York and Boston are barely two hundred miles apart. In parts of Texas, people will drive that distance for dinner. In America's infancy, New York and Boston were very much on the same team, colonial allies in fighting the British. Boston, through most of that early American period, was seen as the more prominent, superior, and civilized city—richer in culture, literature, commerce, and, according to some, even cuisine.

"Boston's clipper ships were faster; its institutions of higher learning were more famous," argues Johnson. "And its chowder was better! Whoever heard of throwing clams into tomato soup?"

But things changed. Dramatically. New York's explosive growth, it turned out, wasn't tied to sailing ships, or schools, much less an alternative style of making clam chowder. Location, it turns out, really is everything. New York City sat on an extraordinary natural harbor, and Manhattan island's geography and geology allowed for immense and sustained development. By 1800, the city had become—and would remain—a center of finance, a vital port of trade and entry for immigrants, and the most populous city in America.

Boston would have to be content with hungrier bookworms and better chowder.

With its ethos of learning, literature, and the liberal arts, "The Hub," as it became known, would take on the role of a modern

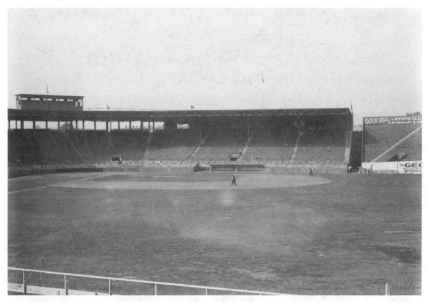

Fenway Park interior, 1914 LIBRARY OF CONGRESS

Fenway Park exterior, circa 1915 LIBRARY OF CONGRESS

Athens, to bigger, bolder New York City's latter-day Sparta. With some historically predictable results. As the original Spartans could attest (undefeated vs. Athens in Peloponnesian League play), brawn frequently wins out over brains. What's particularly ironic is that the manner in which their status as cities changed—New York City eventually leapfrogging over Boston—was uncannily mirrored in baseball.

From 1901 to 1918, Boston was the one of the most dominant teams in baseball. It won the first World Series in 1903 (as the "Americans"—the switch to the Sox came in 1908), and took four more titles between 1912 (the year Fenway Park opened) and 1918.

"Early on, Boston ruled the baseball world," says Johnson. "The call was, 'Break up the Bostons!'"

Incredibly, the Sox saved their competitors the trouble. They broke the team up themselves. The team's owner, Harry Frazee, was a bit of a bon-vivant who needed financing for a Broadway musical, *No, No Nanette*. He found it in Yankee's owner Jacob Rupert. Just after Christmas, 1919, Boston's Babe Ruth was purchased by the Yankees for $100,000. Personally, I've always found some small solace in the fact that at least *No, No Nanette* was a hit, and not a flop. But the Babe was an even bigger hit in New York, and the deal is now regarded by many to be the most fateful (and boneheaded) one in the history of professional sports. Frazee also sold off or traded away other Sox players to the Yankees, but it was the Ruth deal that seemed to crystallize the remarkable reversal of fortunes that soon took hold. In New York, Ruth became a legendary and larger-than-life (his oversized appetites helped) celebrity, Yankee Stadium became known as "the house that Ruth built," and the Yankees first took on their identity as modern America's first glamorous sports powerhouse. Teamed with such stars as Waite Hoyt, Tony Lazzeri, and Lou Gehrig, Ruth headlined the famed "Murderers

Red Sox, World Series, 1912 LIBRARY OF CONGRESS

Row" of the World Champion 1927 Yankees, considered by many to be the greatest single-season baseball team of all time. Ruth, who would retire as the most celebrated slugger and most iconic player in baseball history, single-handedly laid the foundation in New York for what became baseball's—and indeed, all of professional sports'—most famous and enduring dynasty.

The Red Sox, around this same period of time, fared, um, differently.

In 1927, for example, the Sox finished in last place for the third straight season. They would not even *reach*

The man who traded the Babe: Harry Frazee
LIBRARY OF CONGRESS

GEORGE HERMAN
(BABE) RUTH

BIG LEAGUE CHEWING GUM

Babe Ruth chewing gum card
LIBRARY OF CONGRESS

another World Series for nearly thirty years, and it would be eighty-six years before they'd win their first World Championship since 1918. In that same general period of time, the Yankees won *twenty* championship titles. Needless to say, in time, getting rid of Babe Ruth came to be regarded as something akin to the Red Sox's original sin. Over the years, "the Curse of the Bambino," as it's been dubbed, was held responsible not only for Boston's decades of failing to win another championship, but also for the sometimes spectacular and truly excruciating ways they seemed to lose. (Yes, we will get to Bill Buckner.) In truth, there was no curse, although there was never any shortage of believers in it. In 2003, after Boston's devastating Game 7 loss to the Yankees in the eleventh inning of the American League Championship series, New York owner George Steinbrenner chortled to reporters, "The Curse still lives! I sure do believe it now!" (As if to validate that, stunned Sox manager Grady Little pouted sourly, "There are ghosts.")

In truth, what Boston seemed more often cursed with was not the supernatural, but a simple lack of superior pitching. Alas, what they didn't lack was a run of similarly underwhelming managers, and an overly clubby ownership that seemed as nonplussed about finishing last in the standings as it did being dead last in integrating their team. Indeed, any supposed "curse" might also have been named after superstars Jackie Robinson or Willie Mays, both

Babe Ruth (left), Boston dugout, 1916 LIBRARY OF CONGRESS

of whom Boston declined to sign early in their careers. I guess, because, you know, what would you do with Willie Mays?

"For goodness sake," says Johnson, "the *Bruins* had a black player in 1957 [Willie O'Ree] two years before the Red Sox!"

It should also be pointed out that, during the Sox's long years in the desert of futility, it wasn't just the Yankees that bedeviled them. Other teams also broke Boston's hearts in big postseason games, the tragic tales of which were handed down to succeeding generations like the retellings of momentous battles and humiliating defeats, all of which had forced their forebears into endless seasons of fruitless wandering, frustration, and exile. Athletics, Indians, Tigers, Cardinals, Mets—all occupy gut-wrenching places in Boston's pantheon of pain. For nearly a century, the scar tissue on Sox fans' hearts built up progressively, like the concentric rings around the base of a giant redwood: *Here's 1946 . . . there's '67 . . . '78—oh, and that really thick, still-fresh one? Gotta be '86.*

But from the start, one foe has figured more prominently and more symbolically than anyone else. For Sox fans, the New York

Who wins? Young DiMaggio and Williams at the Stadium
NATIONAL BASEBALL HALL OF FAME LIBRARY, COOPERSTOWN, NY

Yankees not only personify the decades of frustration and misery, but also ironically (again) are today the foe that is most linked to Boston's ultimate break with its painful past.

Curiously, although the two teams go back with each other for over a century, "the Rivalry" as it is understood today only gained real steam in the 1940s, and reached its most potent phase only about thirty years ago. In the early 1940s, with the rise of the Red Sox's Ted Williams and the Yankees' Joe DiMaggio, both teams could boast an equivalent "player for the ages," with both in their primes. The 1941 season is famous for Williams chasing a .400 batting average, while DiMaggio chased the game's longest hitting streak. (Williams finished with a .406 average, while DiMaggio's streak ran to fifty-six games; both records still stand.) The Yankees won the pennant; the Sox finished second. But the sense of rivalry, fueled by the dueling superstars' separate quests, became real and palpable for a new generation. Five years later, the Sox found themselves the pennant winners, but hard-luck losers (naturally) to the St. Louis Cardinals in the World Series. In 1948, under former Yankees manager Joe McCarthy, Boston seemed poised to win another pennant, but ended up finishing tied for first with the Cleveland Indians, who then defeated the Sox in a one-game play-off. (The loss, alas, also nixed what would have been an all-Boston World Series with the then–National League Boston Braves.)

"One time we could have had the Yanks," laments Richard Johnson. "The Sox finally had the Yankees on a downslide, and the *Indians* rise up!"

Imagine. On top of the inconvenience for Boston in having to occasionally deal with other, upstart foes, New York's "downslides" were, typically, brief. By the end of the 1940s, the Sox-Yankees rivalry had entered a lull. Mostly because the Yankees had become, quite simply, unrivaled. (Not that Boston didn't have plenty of

Joe DiMaggio salutes his bat, 1941. LIBRARY OF CONGRESS

Fenway Park, pre-Green Monster seats LIBRARY OF CONGRESS

company in resentment and frustration: it was a long-suffering fan of the Washington Senators—not the Red Sox—who, desperate to beat New York, made a deal with the devil in the 1955 Broadway hit *Damn Yankees*.) In the thirteen years from 1949 to 1962, the Yankees won nine World Series titles, including *five in a row*. Over the same period, the Red Sox would fail to finish above second place, all of which leads to a logical question that inevitably gnawed at many Sox fans of a certain age: can it really be a rivalry if only one rival ever really wins? (To wit, some observers—particularly from New York—have described "the Rivalry" as being as real as the one between a hammer and a nail.)

"Honestly, there are times when it seems more like an abusive relationship," observes Gordon Edes, a veteran sportswriter who covers baseball for ESPN Boston, and who was a longtime Red Sox beat writer for the *Boston Globe*.

As Edes sees it, New York's perennial dominance on the diamond only rubbed salt in a wound that Boston had been left to lick a long time ago, having been eclipsed as a city by New York.

"Let's face it, what fuels the rivalry from the New England side is a very healthy inferiority complex."

While Freud at Fenway could no doubt find plenty to analyze, it was instead the 1967 season that gave a therapeutic boost to Boston's self-esteem, and ushered in a new era for the underdog Sox.

The previous season (1966) had seen Boston finish ninth in the (then) ten-team American League.

There was a silver lining, though: the Sox finished ahead of the Yankees, who, having spent themselves in the final, parting fireworks of Maris and Mantle, were about to descend, like all those tape-measure homerun balls, back to earth. New York would not recover its first-place form for a decade.

For Boston, 1967 will forever be remembered as "the Impossible Dream" season. The Red Sox started the season with a new manager (Dick Williams), but jaundiced Boston observers expected to see the same old results. The Sox had become known as a "country club" team. "Twenty-five men, twenty-five cabs" was how others described the team—little cohesion, little color (figuratively and literally), little pitching or hitting, but lots of well-paid, low-producing stiffs going through the motions. (A poster child of the period? First-baseman Dick Stuart. Guy could hit. Fielding? His nickname was "Dr. Strangeglove.")

But something happened. Maybe it was partly the no-nonsense style of their new skipper. Maybe it was the addition of new blood, like the slugging and slick-fielding new first baseman George "Boomer" Scott, or fleet new centerfielder Reggie Smith. But mostly it was the way the Sox jelled as a hard-charging team, and rode the coattails of Carl "Yaz" Yastrzemski (who had inherited left field from Ted

Williams) and his spectacular Triple-Crown season. Boston won the American League pennant on the last day of the season. Alas, waiting for them once again in the World Series were the St. Louis Cardinals (winners in 1946), who, once again, beat Boston in seven games.

This time, however, Boston seem to awake from the Impossible Dream season seemingly a different franchise than the one that had been essentially sleep-walking through most of the previous twenty years. The team was newly energized, more competitive, and the fans flocked to Fenway like never before. Home attendance in 1968 (nearly 2 million) set a new season record, and the Sox haven't dropped below the million mark since. The fervent, far-flung (nationwide) fan base known today as Red Sox Nation was but a fledgling republic in 1968. The "Sweet Caroline"-ing, kneejerk nationalism (complete with pink hats) had yet to take hold. But it was all born in the afterglow of the Impossible Dream.

Partly, the notion of a "nation" to begin with has as much to do with geography as it does with loyalty. The Sox are the only major league baseball team among the six states (Massachusetts, Maine, New Hampshire, Vermont, Connecticut, Rhode Island) that make up New England. So they're deeply identified with a region as well as a city, and have always been very much "New England's" baseball team. To a point. A point on the compass, that is.

The one other major league baseball team that claims considerable clutches of committed fans in New England is—surprise, surprise—the Yankees. New York is, after all, the only other state that borders New England, and the Yankees are the closest neighboring big league team.

"I mean, the two metropolitan areas are so close together, we all know people in both areas," points out Richard Johnson. "Everyone has their uncle Phil the Yankees fan, who's always ribbing about the Red Sox."

While there are certainly Yankee fans (and assorted "Uncle Phils") scattered throughout New England, with sizeable pockets of them in both Vermont and the Berkshires of western Massachusetts (Jim Bouton's backyard), the border of Red Sox nation becomes most porous in southern Connecticut. While unmarked and unpatrolled (not to mention unsecured), the border does have an official name: the Munson-Nixon Line.

It's a play on the famed Mason-Dixon Line (the popularly accepted demarcation for the northern and southern American states), and refers to a Yankee catcher, the late Thurman Munson, and retired Red Sox outfielder Trot Nixon. It was coined in 2003 by *Sports Illustrated* writer Steve Rushin in a column titled, "Resident Alien in Red Sox Nation," in which Rushin describes moving from Manhattan to Massachusetts, and his ensuing sense of dislocation as a baseball fan. ("Manhattan and New England," Rushin writes, "share a currency but not a clam chowder. Nor much of anything else.") The unofficial boundary, notes Rushin, runs "north of New Haven but south of Hartford, running the breadth of central Connecticut . . . below which you love Thurman, above which you love Trot."

(In 2014, the *New York Times*, in cooperation with Facebook, used detailed, aggregated data to create what it called an "unprecedented look at the geography of baseball fandom" across America, "down to the "Zip Code Level." In doing so, it was able to take the guesswork out of Rushin's original thesis, and precisely plot the city-by-city, town-by-town meandering of the Munson-Nixon Line, as well as the exact percentages of Yankees and Red Sox support in each locale. Turns out my hometown of Winthrop, Massachusetts—which borders Boston, mind you—includes 10 percent Yankee fans. Oh, the shame.)

As it happens, no Yankee player more passionately embodied the spirit of the Rivalry than Thurman Munson. (In 1979, at

Thurman Munson, The Look NATIONAL BASEBALL HALL OF FAME LIBRARY, COOPERSTOWN, NY

thirty-two, Munson died tragically in a private plane crash in Ohio.) Famed for his fiery temperament on the field, Munson played his entire eleven-year, All-Star career with New York, during a decade in which the Yankees not only won two more World Series titles,

Carlton Fisk: spring training, circa 1970

but also seemed to cement their contentious relationship with the Red Sox. The 1970s were, in some ways, the golden age of the Sox-Yankees rivalry. Although, considering some of the actual jousting and hand-to-hand combat that occurred, perhaps the period was more like the Middle Ages.

Munson's counterpart on the Red Sox was Boston's equally talented—and equally fiery—catcher, Carlton "Pudge" Fisk. The pride of Charlestown, New Hampshire, Fisk played for twenty-four years (the last twelve with the Chicago White Sox) and was inducted into Baseball's Hall of Fame in 2000. When he retired in 1993, Fisk held the all-time home record for homeruns by a catcher (351). Both he (1972) and Munson (1970) were named American League Rookie of the Year. Both were considered the heart and soul and field general of their respective teams. (Munson had been named the Yankees first team captain since Lou Gehrig.) And, as one would expect of two military leaders whose armies are at war, neither one was on the other's Christmas card list.

"Substitute Joe (DiMaggio) and Ted (Williams) with Munson and Fisk," says Richard Johnson. "But Joe and Ted did not hate each other."

Munson and Fisk?

"They hated each other!" bellows former Yankee relief pitcher and Hall-of-Famer Rich "Goose" Gossage, on the phone from his home in Colorado. After the birth of his first son, Gossage got a chance to see just how deep that hostility went.

"We named him 'Jeffrey Carlton Gossage'" relates Gossage. "We just liked the name, 'Carlton', was all. Munson never forgave me. He yelled at me, 'How could you *do* that?'"

Munson and Fisk first tangled directly in a 1973 home-plate collision. Munson, running toward home plate, slammed into Fisk, who held onto the ball and, as an added flourish, kicked Munson off of him and into the air. The benches emptied. Tensions simmered, bad blood remained, and the Rivalry seemed to have been reignited—with Fisk and Munson seemingly happy to fan the flames.

"Fisk and Munson did not like each other," emphasizes former Red Sox pitcher Bill Lee. "They really just didn't like each other, and that affected both teams, and it made the Rivalry that much stronger."

It certainly affected Bill Lee.

On the night of May 20, 1976, New York was leading Boston 1-0 in the sixth inning at Yankee Stadium.

In yet another close play at the plate, New York's Lou Piniella ran headlong into Fisk, who again held onto the ball and, again, came up swinging. Again, the benches emptied, but this time, knots of players continued to brawl all over the infield. Lefthander Lee, who had been sucker-punched from behind by New York's Mickey Rivers, tried to retaliate, but was thrown to the ground by Yankee third-baseman Graig Nettles.

"Then he stomped on my shoulder," Lee recounts today. "I jumped up and thought I threw a left hook, but my arm didn't move; that's when I knew something was wrong."

Lee sustained torn ligaments and was sidelined for five weeks. Didn't really matter. The Sox ended up finishing 15.5 games behind the Yankees, who lost to the Cincinnati Reds in the World Series. (The same Reds team that had beaten the Sox in the previous year's World Series.) In 1977, the Yankees roared back to win the World Series against the Dodgers. But a year later (1978), Boston seemed to have turned the tables. The Yankees were beset with internal strife, as manager Billy Martin, star slugger Reggie Jackson, and owner George Steinbrenner all feuded publicly, and engaged in what seemed like a season-long soap opera. (Martin quit during the season.) Meanwhile, the Red Sox rolled. By mid-July, they led the Yankees by fourteen games.

And then, all of a sudden, they didn't. The Red Sox went into a tailspin. The Yankees found their footing. In early September, they came into Fenway Park trailing the Sox by four games. What followed has been dubbed "the Boston Massacre." Four games later, the Yankees had swept the Sox by an aggregate score of 42-9, and left town tied for first place.

"'78 was such a killer," says Gordon Edes. "Reggie and Billy were fighting with each other and it looks like the Sox will finally put their foot on the Yankees' neck for a change—and then an epic collapse."

But then, what other kind of collapse would the Sox have?

A month later, the season ended with the bitter rivals tied for first, forcing a rare one-game playoff on October 2, 1978, at Fenway Park. (Boston had won a coin toss.)

"Weirdest atmosphere I've ever experienced in baseball, even before we took the field," recalls Gossage vividly. "There was a buzz in that park, like a low hum, created by the fans. It wasn't raucous; it was quiet, almost eerie; some of us commented to each other, 'Listen to that.' I've never heard it before or since. They knew the magnitude of the game."

The afternoon game began on a classic, cool, sun-dappled day, where autumn's lengthening and sharp shadows lay across the outfield like dark, jagged fissures in the still-bright green grass. And for nearly seven innings, the Sox seemed to find a way not to fall in, and to tiptoe steadily ahead. For nearly seven innings.

"It was so intense, such an amazing game," says Gossage, who pitched three innings that day. "I remember standing on the mound at one point and actually thinking, 'It's too bad one team has to lose this game.'"

Rich "Goose" Gossage NATIONAL BASEBALL HALL OF FAME LIBRARY, COOPERSTOWN, NY

In the seventh, with one-out, a three-run homer by New York's Bucky Dent put the Yankees up 3-2. They would go on to win the game (5-4), and to eventually win the World Series, where Dent was named the MVP. Across New England, Sox fans did their own renaming: Russell Earl "Bucky" Dent has become forever known as Bucky "Bleeping" Dent. (One could ask why the Sox pitcher who served up the homerun never got renamed "Mike Bleeping Torrez," but perhaps dealers of fateful pitches suffer enough. Ask Ralph Branca.)

For a while, the air seemed to go out of the Sox. And the Rivalry. In 1986, Boston did find its way back to a pennant, and the World Series. Against New York, too. But it was the Mets, not the Yankees, and for Sox fans, the less that is recalled and recounted about that truly traumatic experience, the better. It's like bringing up a family tragedy whose sad and painful memory is something people have spent decades trying to blot out and forget. For those who lived it, watching video of the slow-rolling ball squirting through gimpy Bill Buckner's legs, and with it, the game, is a bit like watching the grainy, black and white footage of the Zapruder film. One is tempted to look away. Still.

In 1986, future Red Sox pitcher Tim Wakefield was a college student. He watched the fateful Game 6 with his roommate, a Sox fan from Connecticut.

"It was, like, horrifying," Wakefield recalls today. "He smashed something, and I realized, wow, this goes pretty deep. Yeah, I had a sense of the history right then."

Seventeen years later, in a stunning twist of irony, Wakefield, who retired in 2011, would have reason to recall the Red Sox horror of 1986 in a very personal way. It would involve former Yankee third baseman Aaron Boone, who himself had a forewarning of what life in the midst of the Rivalry could be like. Midway through

Tim Wakefield NATIONAL BASEBALL HALL OF FAME LIBRARY, COOPERSTOWN, NY

the 2003 season, Boone was traded from the National League Cincinnati Reds to the Yankees. As Boone packed up his things and said goodbye to teammates, the Reds' Tim Naehring—a former Red Sox third baseman—stepped into the clubhouse.

"Tim leaned down and said, 'Let me tell you something,'" Boone recalls. "'You have no idea what you're in for.'"

But in the late fall of 1986, in the wake of the shattering loss at Shea Stadium, all across an ashen Red Sox Nation, a new generation began to believe in the Bambino's curse. I mean, how could there not be *something*? How could a team continue to find such inexplicable, unimaginable, truly *excruciating* ways to lose? And how could it possibly get any worse?

How, indeed.

The 1990s were at least a competitive period again for both Boston and New York. In 1999, the rivals faced each other in the American League Championship series. The winner would go on to the World Series. The Yankees went on to the World Series (as they did the year before, as they would do the following two years as well).

In 2003, the Yankees finished in first place. The second-place Sox made the playoffs as the American League Wild Card team. In the Division Series, the Yankees easily dispatched the Minnesota Twins. The Sox just did get by the Athletics, setting the stage for the rivals to meet again in the American League Championship Series with, once more, a pennant and a trip to the World Series on the line.

The anticipated drama didn't disappoint. Nor did the renewed intensity of the rivalry. A century's worth of New York dominance and Boston frustration had rubbed things to a raw edge. In the Fenway Park stands, "Yankees Suck!" was as ubiquitous a cry as "Popcorn!" or "Hot dogs!" At the stadium, meanwhile, Yankee fans taunted back with a much more knowing and finely turned knife: "19-18," was all they had to chant in savage singsong, at once returning fire and reminding Boston just how long it had been since they had last won a World Series.

"It was really like a heavyweight title fight," says Aaron Boone. "We just kept killing each other and killing each other—and it's hard to kill 'em!"

Seesawing between Boston and New York, both teams scratched and clawed their way to a full seven games. On the night of October 16, at Yankee Stadium, Sox ace Pedro Martinez faced former Sox star Roger Clemens in the final, deciding game. The Red Sox looked locked in; they led 5-2 in the bottom of the eighth. But Martinez was tiring. Boston manager Grady Little elected, against all the facts before him, to leave his ace in. Wrong move. When Little did finally close the barn door and call the bullpen, the horses were gone and the score was tied. It stayed that way until the bottom of the eleventh. Sox knuckleballer Tim Wakefield (who had pitched a scoreless tenth) faced the inning's first Yankee batter, Boone. One pitch, and it was over. Homerun. It was as if the Red Sox were now living baseball's version of "Groundhog Day." It was as if the never-changing script was now engraved on some sort of stone tablet of the baseball gods: details of time, place, pitcher, and inning could be altered for variety, but the ultimate result neither could nor would ever vary. Like it was somehow ordained: *twas ever thus, and so it shall be for evermore.*

As jubilant Yankees celebrated on the field behind him, Tim Wakefield made his way, head down, toward the Sox dugout. He was thirty-seven years old, and an eight-year Sox veteran. But his mind raced back to another night many years ago, and a game he watched as a young college student—a game that also ended with a horrific Red Sox loss.

"As I walked off," Wakefield recalls, "my first thought was, I'm the new Bill Buckner."

Some observers thought maybe this loss, owing to where it was and to whom, was even worse.

"As devastating a scene in a losing locker room as I have ever seen," recalls Gordon Edes. "Sox owner John Henry was in a black trenchcoat, making his rounds from player to player, like the Angel of Death himself."

Having turned off the TV, and sitting in my now-darkened family room, my own thoughts turned somewhat to the supernatural, too. Boston's loss this night was so supreme, so thoroughly devastating, so gruesomely bound up with its longtime nemesis, and yet in the end so classically predictable, that it conjured more Greek mythology than American pastime. For the Sox, it seemed now there was only one path to redemption: to return, in one year—the very next season—to the very same stage, and at long last, vanquish their tormentor right here, in his own home. Now, nothing less would do.

Nothing could seem as unlikely. A baseball season is long and notoriously unpredictable. And yet ... that's nothing short of exactly what happened.

Almost as soon as the 2003 season ended, both the Yankees and Red Sox made moves to bolster their teams. For the rivals, one could sense that this off season was about re-arming, reloading, and digging in for what Boston fervently—desperately— hoped would be a chance for a rematch. The Sox added All-Star pitcher Curt Schilling; the Yankees acquired superstar slugger Alex Rodriguez (foiling Boston's attempt to sign him). By mid-season 2004, Boston had already fallen eight games behind New York. Nonetheless, it was clear that the level of hostility was as high as ever. On July 24 at Fenway, the Red Sox fought back from five runs down to beat the Yankees. But it was a for-real fight on the first-base line that still stands out. In an ironic twist on the Fisk-Munson battle thirty years earlier, Boston's catcher and captain, Jason Varitek, jousted with the Yanks' Rodriguez. Seemingly re-invigorated (and having traded their own star, Nomar Garciaparra), the Sox ended the regular season within three games of the first-place Yankees.

Both teams promptly dispatched their first-round playoff opponents. Now, one year later, incredibly and against all odds, the 2004 American League Championship Series would feature an exact rematch of the fiery and unforgettable 2003 series. The Red Sox would get their shot at redemption after all.

But (three letters that have clung to the Sox as closely as "R-E-D"), three games into the series, the Redemption Tour bus was all but in a ditch, wheels spinning in air, dazed passengers walking in circles around it, wondering what had gone so terribly wrong. The first two games had been competitive enough, with the Sox within three runs of the Yankees at the end (the losing end, that is) of each game. In Game 3, alas, all pretense of a fair fight evaporated, as Boston's tires—and arms—blew out. New York scored *nineteen* runs, and for the Red Sox now, nothing but the final ditch lay ahead, where high hopes would yet again be laid low, and where "the curse," far from being buried, would instead be laid like a cruel wreath on another sickening Sox collapse.

And then, it happened: Pigs flew. Hell froze over. The nail hit the hammer. The Sox stopped the Yankees. This time, up from the familiar ditch of about-to-be-buried dreams, redemption, for once, wriggled free.

The odds of the Red Sox doing what they did next were not merely staggering; they were, in a real sense, nonexistent. It had never been done in the history of Major League Baseball.

Down 0-3 in the best-of-seven series and facing elimination at Fenway in Game 4 (and each subsequent game), Boston bore down and kept the score close. In the ninth inning, down 4-3, they managed to tie the game on a single off of perhaps the greatest relief pitcher ever, Mariano Rivera. To do it, and to have gotten himself into critical scoring position, pinch runner Dave Roberts pulled off what is now the most famous stolen base in Boston's history. In the eleventh (that fateful inning again), slugger David "Big Papi" Ortiz began burnishing his legacy as the greatest postseason hitter since—naturally, New York's—Reggie Jackson. A dramatic, walk-off, two-run homerun, and the Sox had managed to win 6-4 and to stay alive in the series. It was after midnight, and the Sox, like Lazarus, were stirring.

Game 5 began at Fenway, later that same calendar day (Monday, October 18) at 5:11 p.m. EDT. Again, the two teams battled, cinched, and pummeled, drawing blood, but neither team was able to open up a lead they could keep. And so it went, white-knuckle-like, into the fourteenth inning. When, once again, for the second time in the *same day*, David Ortiz strode confidently to the plate, lined a two-run, walk-off single to centerfield, and strode off, swarmed by his delirious teammates. Both Red Sox and Yankees, players and fans alike, seemed to suddenly be having the same jangled thought: "This is not happening."

But it was.

Game 6 shifted to New York and Yankee Stadium. Curt Schilling started for the Sox, in what has become known as the "Bloody Sock" game. Schilling had been gritting it out in the series, trying to continue to pitch with a painful tendon injury in his right ankle. During the course of the game, the white part of his right sock became as blood-red-stained as the red part. It was a memorable, gutsy performance, with Schilling holding onto a Sox lead

Yankee Stadium, the original LIBRARY OF CONGRESS

through seven innings. Boston got some crucial calls their way as well, prompting New York fans to fling debris on the field, and New York police in full riot gear to come out and take up protective positions. (Only between the Yankees and the Red Sox could a baseball playoff game take on the armor-wearing, taser-toting elements of an actual urban SWAT scene.) Order was maintained long enough to give New York fans a reason to really want to fling something. Like themselves off of the GW Bridge. Boston won the game 4-2, and became the first team in the history of Major League Baseball playoffs to tie a series after being down 0-3.

Before the deciding Game 7 in New York began on Wednesday, October 20, in a symbolic gesture that was equal parts clever and cruel, the Yankees had Bucky Dent throw out the ceremonial first pitch. This time, however, on this night, some sort of cosmic statute of limitations seemed to have been lifted. It was okay to stake out a lead against your most feared and hated foe, and keep it, and not squander or blow it, and finally triumph. Triumph like no Red Sox team and, indeed, no team in all of baseball history had ever done. Nearly one year to the day since Tim Wakefield had walked off the field at Yankee Stadium in shocked defeat, his mind this time raced in a different way, as he ran out to join his jumping, joyful teammates.

"It really was just the most supreme irony," Wakefield marvels. "One year later, and there I was, getting to celebrate on the same exact field."

Irony, on this night, cut in both directions. Yankee fans, seemingly too numb to move, could only sit in silence, gaping at the scene before them in utter disbelief. After all the decades of Yankee dominance and victorious celebrations here, this was perhaps the most jarring and ignominious defeat imaginable. A historic collapse for the ages. Not even on the road, but right here in The House That Ruth Built. And before the very team that had sent Ruth here to begin with.

For some Yankees, even a decade later, what happened in the 2004 ALCS still hasn't fully sunk in.

"I'm still in denial," says Goose Gossage.

In 2004, with the Yankees up three games to none against the Red Sox, Gossage went off with friends into the Colorado wilderness on a hunting trip. Days later, he came out of the woods, went into a store, asked confidently who the Yanks were playing in the World Series, and was told check out the TV in the back room—where he was stunned to see the Sox about to win the clinching Game 4 at Yankee Stadium.

"I swear I'm still in denial. I am still trying to figure out how they did that."

While it felt mildly anticlimactic, the Sox did, of course, face a final hurdle before they could fully throw the supposed "curse" monkey off their back. To do it, they extended the four-game winning streak that had begun against the Yankees to eight. On October 27, 2004, Boston completed a four-game sweep of the St. Louis Cardinals to win their first World Series title since 1918.

And the Rivalry?

Like baseball itself, it goes on; it changes; it endures. The Red Sox, having endured an eighty-six-year championship drought, seemed inclined to keep slaking their built-up thirst. They won the World Series again in 2007 (vs. Colorado) and 2013 (vs. St. Louis). The Yankees, as of 2015, were still waiting to win a title in the twenty-first century. When the two teams play now, the raw edge seems dulled. There may be taunting and booing, but it seems forced now, and more for effect than from any need to settle scores.

"Oh, yeah, it's changed, very much so," observes Bill Lee. "They're not throwing real punches anymore like we did."

Indeed, on both teams, it's almost as if something that festered for so long has been lanced. The players themselves now seem to carry no real grudges.

"It's not as intense as the 70s, not the same outright hatred as Fisk and Munson," says Tim Wakefield. "When Jeter retired, that seemed like the end of this generation of the Rivalry. It's at a lull right now, a generational gap right now."

"It's certainly not as intense as it once was," says Gordon Edes. "But do I think the Rivalry is dead? Not a chance. It'll come back."

In other quarters, it's never ended.

As we wrap up a conversation on the phone, former Yankee Jim Bouton seems to forget he lives in Massachusetts, but eagerly remembers he's talking with someone in Boston.

"I had a great record against Boston; look it up—it was like 13-5," he says gleefully. "I always tell Boston reporters or if I'm on the radio with a Boston station—'13-5 lifetime against Boston!'"

Above Yawkey Way, Fenway Park: The title that broke an 86-year drought. (And maybe, possibly, allegedly, a curse.) PHOTO, TED REINSTEIN

On the other hand, one veteran of the Rivalry who has every reason to hold his grudge has, perhaps, mellowed just a wee bit. Sox pitcher Bill Lee, seriously injured when he was thrown to the ground by New York's Graig Nettles in the infamous 1976 melee, for years refused to talk to Nettles, even as he made peace with some of the brawl's other participants. But a few years ago, Lee encountered Nettles at a Little League banquet in Connecticut that they both were attending.

"I saw him sitting at a table by himself, nursing a drink," Lee says. "I walked up to him and I said, 'You know, I always wanted to kill you, but seeing you sitting here with that drink, you just look like an old duvet cover.'"

Not exactly the Paris Peace Treaty. But in the hundred years war that has been the Boston–New York rivalry, it passes for détente. Hardball style.

("The Rivalry"): Brothers in Arms

In New England, a favorite parlor game for Red Sox and Yankee fans involves expounding on the precise, if rambling, route of the famed "Munson-Nixon Line," the six-state region's putative boundary separating Boston red from New York pinstripes. As commonly accepted, the line runs northeast-west across Connecticut: north of the Hartford area you're in Red Sox Nation; south of it, you are more likely to belong to the "Evil Empire," as former Sox president and CEO Larry Lucchino has described the Yankees.

But for Bill and Bob Dowling, the Munson-Nixon Line is more of a moveable thing. For them, it goes where they go. It has to. It's all in the family.

"Mother and father were Sox fans," says Bob Dowling, 68. "It was a genetic thing."

The Dowling boys grew up in the central Massachusetts city of Holyoke. Bob still lives there.

"Hated the Yankees growing up—despised them!" adds Bob's older brother Bill, 73. "I courted my wife at Fenway, was at Fenway for the Bucky Dent game."

That must have been a fun date. But life, like a baseball, can take funny hops.

Bill doesn't live in Holyoke anymore. An attorney, he moved out of state and in 1986 took a job as general counsel for a very prestigious and world-famous company: the New York Yankees.

"Unbelievable, totally unbelievable," snorts Bob Dowling, when asked how he reacted to the news that his big brother was going to work for the Yankees. But he's just getting warmed up.

"It was like he joined Al-Qaeda or something," Bob laughs, reaching playfully for the most extreme metaphor he can come up with. "It was inconceivable! Like he went over to the dark side."

As team counsel, Bill Dowling worked closely for many years with Yankees owner George Steinbrenner. ("More than I ever wanted to," says Dowling.) Both brothers, in separate conversations, are quick to point out that they love each other very much, and can laugh about their divided baseball allegiances.

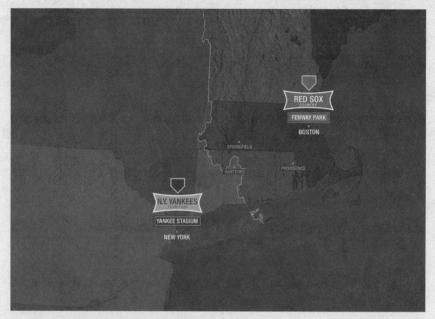

Baseball's most contested border: The Munson-Nixon Line
GRAPHICS COURTESY, WCVB-TV

Sort of.

"Crazy Red Sox fan!" Bill says of his kid brother.

But clearly, it wasn't an easy transition for this Massachusetts-kid-turned-Yankee-big-wig.

"I still felt conflicted when the Sox played the Yankees," he admits. "Eventually I did become a full-fledged Yankees fan." Quickly, however, he adds, "But with two small fs."

Eventually, after leaving the Yankees, Bill Dowling found the perfect way to bridge the two baseball worlds he and his brother straddled: by finding a neutral one. In 2000, he bought the minor-league New Britain (CT) Rock Cats and became the club's managing partner and president.

"I was in my 50's, and had always loved baseball," says Dowling. "I wanted to do something fun!"

Bill Dowling also immediately reached out to his younger brother, retired only a month, to become the team's media director.

"Brothers in Arms": Bill and Bob Dowling, New Britain, CT
PHOTO, COURTESY BOB DOWLING

"He said to me, 'You must be bored by now!,'" laughs Bob Dowling.

A Boston affiliate until 1995, New Britain was in the Minnesota Twins organization under the Dowlings' ownership—which is just as well. New Britain, Connecticut, lies perilously close to being dead center of the Munson-Nixon Line, almost exactly halfway between New York City and Boston.

In 2002, with Major League Baseball considering contraction, there was the possibility that New Britain would no longer be aligned with the Twins.

"I got a call from a season-ticket holder," recalls Bill Dowling. "He said, 'If you ever become a Yankees affiliate, I will cancel my tickets.'

A short time later, I got another call—'If you ever become a Red Sox affiliate. . . .' That's the way it was in New Britain, right down the middle, half and half."

Bob Dowling sounds more like he is describing the UN than a ball club.

"We referred to ourselves as the 'Switzerland of baseball,'" he laughs. "Neutral and right in the middle."

The brothers owned and ran the team for twelve years. (The Rock Cats have since moved to Hartford and are now known as the Yard Goats.) They remain very close today, though Bill has remained in Connecticut, and Bob in Massachusetts. With all their brotherly love and years of working together, they're not beyond ribbing each other over their still-divided baseball loyalties. For Bob, there's the searing memory of those free tickets, and his boys accompanying their Uncle Bill to games at Yankee Stadium.

"He'd bring them into the clubhouse; they'd sit on Willie Randolph's lap—my youngest son even became a *Yankees fan* for a period!"

Bob Dowling pauses for dramatic effect, letting the horrific memory subside.

"We had to get him deprogrammed; fortunately he's back in the fold now."

Ever the mature older brother and diplomat, Bill Dowling is inclined to focus on the positive, and the present.

"I've mellowed a bit," he admits. "Let's just say that when the Sox finally won the World Series, I wasn't unhappy."

Mellow, indeed, coming from a Yankees fan.

("The Rivalry"): Muddle over Mudville

More acclaimed writing and literature has been devoted to baseball, by far, than any other sport. Not surprising, since baseball is both America's pastime and, along with jazz, its greatest invention. (Granted, as inventions go, the airplane, the personal computer, and the polio vaccine weren't too shabby, either.) Some truly gifted writers have written about baseball, such as John Updike, Bernard Malamud, David Halberstam, W. P. Kinsella, Ring Lardner, Roger Angell, and Roger Kahn, just to name a few. Ernest L. Thayer is not a name generally included with these. And yet, his singular contribution to baseball's literary canon is perhaps the most famous of all, and the only one that is both widely quotable and instantly recognizable. After all, who isn't familiar with "Casey at the Bat"?

Thayer's celebrated poem was first published on June 3, 1888, by the *San Francisco Daily Examiner*. A Massachusetts native, Thayer had moved to California to work for the newspaper, which was owned by the family of his former Harvard classmate, William Randolph Hearst. While "Casey" did not become famous immediately, it certainly did within a year or so of its publication, helped by public performances by stage celebrities of the time, like New York's DeWolf Hopper. (The poem was published originally under the pseudonym "Phin," short for Thayer's college nickname, "Phinney.")

Thayer died in Santa Barbara, California, in 1940. But two questions have long remained about his most famous work: was there a real-life Casey, and similarly, was Mudville inspired by a real place? On the "Casey" question, Thayer wrote, "The only Casey actually involved, I am sure about him, was a big, dour Irish lad of my high school days." And Mudville? Stockton, California, is quite sure that it is the inspiration for the home of history's most famous strikeout. "Nice try," says Holliston, Massachusetts, which will tell you with equal certainty that it, not Stockton, is the real-life Mudville.

Both places are able to make solid arguments, which they make without hesitation—or cessation.

"We know this is Mudville," says Holliston town historian Joanne Hulbert flatly. "We know it is."

A town of about fourteen thousand, Holliston sits some twenty-three miles southwest of Boston. I had heard about the Mudville claim soon after moving there in 2001. It's hard to miss the references: there's the "Mudville" sandwich at the Superette (corned beef, sauerkraut, Swiss, and Russian), Casey's Pub, and the seven-foot carved, wooden "Casey" statue in the low-lying section of town long prone to flooding called— sure enough—Mudville. In 2003, only a few blocks from Holliston's Mudville neighborhood, I chatted with Hulbert.

"Baseball was big in Mudville, especially back in the 1870s, which was about the time that 'Casey' was written," she pointed out. "Thayer loved baseball, his family were woolen manufacturers, and lo and behold, there was a woolen factory in Holliston that was run by one of his relatives. So it's very likely he could have come through here."

Stockton is unfazed.

"Stockton was called 'Mudville,' too," points out Mike Fitzgerald, longtime columnist for the *Stockton Record*. "This place is a river delta and used to get the bejesus flooded out of it—we are a muddier Mudville, I guarantee you!"

Fitzgerald has a point. A city of just over 300,000 on the San Joaquin River, Stockton was known as "Slough City" because of its muddy thoroughfares. It was also a thriving baseball town. And while Thayer may or may not have ever visited Holliston, he quite likely did cover some baseball in Stockton for the *Examiner,* which did, after all, publish his poem.

"Yes, it was a San Francisco paper," concedes Hulbert. "But there's also the case that Thayer wrote the poem while he was back here, and sent it back to Hearst."

Where's instant replay when you really need it?

"A number of the players' names in 'Casey' were not, I don't think, picked out of thin air," says Fitzgerald. "Cooney, Barrows, Blake, Flynn, Cahill—all were actual players in Stockton. I think Stockton simply has the stronger claim."

Obviously, this could go on forever. And it often seems as though it has. For his part, ever the reasonable and objective journalist, Fitzgerald puts his hometown roots aside and points out a rather compelling argument—against *both* Holliston and his own Stockton.

"Mudville vs. Crushers/Amador County's David "Wheels" Alton & Holliston's John "Choo-Choo" Shannahan: Stockton, CA., Aug. 1, 2010

"Thayer himself said it was neither," observes Fitzgerald. "Now, if you can think up an argument why his own statement would be wrong, well. . . ."

It's true. Years after the poem was published, in an interview with a New York newspaper, Thayer said, "The poem has no basis in fact."

But that hasn't stopped the continuing cross-country feud over "Casey." So, in 2010, Fitzgerald had a creative idea, and acted as a peace broker of sorts. He helped arrange for Stockton and Holliston to settle their longstanding (and clearly unresolvable) feud with a duel. On the diamond. In his Sunday column of August 1, 2010, Fitzgerald wrote:

The Mudville Base Ball Club from Holliston, Mass., took the field Saturday while Northern California's Amador County Crushers prepared to hit. Before barely 100 spectators, they began a game aimed at settling two cities' identities and more than a century of history.

The game was played by archaic (nineteenth-century) rules; both teams are "old time baseball" clubs that feature period uniforms, along with assorted beards and mustaches that would have been very familiar to Casey and his Mudville Nine teammates.

The game was not, however, played in neutral territory. While the Holliston club has played games elsewhere on the East Coast and in the Midwest, the Mudville "duel" was played in Stockton. By all accounts, the opposing players seemed more united by a passion for baseball than divided by an age-old argument.

"It was played for the game we love and the hero we share," says John "Choo-Choo" Shannahan, who founded the Holliston club in 2003. "The other guys were great guys, a lot younger than we were! But they were happy and proud to carry the 'Mudville' banner for Stockton."

Maybe Stockton's younger legs made the difference. Maybe it was jet-lag. Or maybe it was just a tough road game. At any rate, Stockton beat Holliston 10-4.

But if the hope was to somehow settle something, the game might as well have ended up in a tie.

"Sure we lost," reasons Shannahan. "But if anything, that give us an even better claim to be the real Mudville!"

All of which suggests that while there may not be outright joy in (this) Mudville, there sure is some major-league persistence.

CHAPTER 6

Politics
(The Hub's Other Hardball)

No DISCUSSION OF FEUDS IN NEW ENGLAND—PARTICULARLY in Boston—would be complete without including politics. That would be like talking about life in the Midwest without mentioning farming. Same thing. Only dirtier.

Nowhere in New England (and few places in America) has politics been a deeper part of the culture and practiced with more passion than in Boston. Indeed, Boston's role in the original colonies' seething, political struggles predates American independence itself. The shrewd tactical minds of John Hancock and Dr. Joseph Warren helped plot a path of rebellion and independence. The lawyerly, rational case for it was brilliantly and eloquently laid out by John Adams. And the fiery oratory of his cousin, Sam Adams, rallied and riled up the citizenry, almost single-handedly inciting the revolution.

Today, Sam Adams's statue stands outside Boston's historic Faneuil Hall. Arms folded in eternal defiance, he stares across the traffic of Congress Street at city hall, where, from his fifth-floor

Old Boston City Hall (1865-1969) LIBRARY OF CONGRESS

office, Boston's mayor can look down and stare back. That's three centuries of Boston politics exchanging glances right there. Politically, the city was a tough room back then (it drove the British out), and it has been ever since. Its reputation for spirited, colorful, and often bare-knuckled (and blood-thirsty) politics is well-deserved, and has long seemed as much a city trademark as baked beans, chowder, and missing Rs.

(To be sure, there are a handful of other cities—New York and Chicago come to mind—where politics is also particularly intense. "But there aren't many on that level," observes former Boston city councilor Larry DiCara. "Try finding some books on the politics of Indiana.")

Former Massachusetts State Representative (14th Suffolk District) and mayoral candidate Jim Brett still marvels at the degree to which politics is in Boston's blood. From birth, it sometimes seems.

"When I was running (for mayor) in '93, I used to marvel that sixth-graders knew all the candidates!" Brett laughs. "It just seems to be part of the DNA here."

What Brett knows as well as anyone is that when some of those sixth-graders grow up and run for office themselves in Boston, the battles can be meaner and more bruising than schoolyard fights.

"No question," says Brett. "Politics is truly a contact sport in Boston."

In fact, within what seems like left-hook range of that same Sam Adams statue stand statues of two other men. Both—James M. Curley and Kevin H. White—were legendary, four-term Boston mayors. Both did indeed, and gleefully, play politics like a contact sport, and ended up with the scars to show for it. Truth is, when it comes to exemplifying the rough and tumble of Boston politics—not to mention some of its most storied political feuds— some notable ex-mayors serve as the most vivid examples of the city's storied political tradition.

Kevin White died in 2012 at the age of eighty-three. Elected when he was only thirty-eight, he served as mayor from 1968 to 1984. He led Boston during some of its most difficult moments, like court-ordered busing (to achieve school desegregation), and the tense days immediately following the murder of Dr. Martin Luther King Jr. (Following King's assassination, White went on stage at the old Boston Garden during a James Brown concert and pleaded for calm; many credit him for helping to spare Boston some of the ensuing riots and unrest that struck other American cities.)

White was also a supremely confident and ambitious politician. He lost his only bid for governor, but in 1972, he was nearly picked as Democratic presidential nominee George McGovern's running mate. It has long been held that then–U.S. senator and fellow Massachusetts Democrat, the late Ted Kennedy, helped scuttle White's bid. (As we'll see, Kennedy-related feuds are at play with more than one of the mayors referenced here.)

White's campaigns, from his first to his last, were noisy, emotional, roller-coaster types of political drama. This was especially true when they involved one of his most frequent sparring partners, city councilor Joseph F. Timilty. But none of their grudge matches were as ugly and nasty as White's campaign for reelection in 1975 against then–state senator Timilty. From the beginning, the candidates were a study in contrasts, from pedigree to personality.

"They hated each other!" recalls Larry DiCara, who was himself running (successfully) for reelection to city council at the time. "It was a culture war, really—White was privileged, went to good schools; Timilty was a marine who never went to college."

White narrowly defeated Timilty, who ran again (unsuccessfully) in 1979. Although Timilty never succeeded in his mayoral quest, his political tutelage would help make a future winner of a rather unlikely member of his team: his driver, a young man named Tom Menino.

Earnest and hardworking, a product of the city's Hyde Park neighborhood, Menino lacked polish, professional accomplishments, a political base, or a degree. In most cases, that would seem a distinctly disadvantaged place from which to launch a political career. But Menino had an uncanny knack for numbers, and an instinctive, natural feel for no-nonsense, know-your-neighbors retail politics. With his shlumpy look and baked-beans-thick Boston accent, he was as refreshingly unvarnished and "real" as a candidate gets, and no one—no one—outworked him. (Although everyone, it can be said, underestimated him.) He won a city council seat in 1983, and within ten years would become the body's president. In March 1993, President Bill Clinton named then–Boston mayor Ray Flynn to become ambassador to the Vatican. In advance of the fall elections, Tom Menino became acting mayor.

Sizing up the field before entering the race, state representative Jim Brett recalls "not seeing any candidate that would have made me think twice about not running—including Tom Menino."

Today, Brett smiles in wonder and amusement at what he—and a whole city—could not have known then. The man who mocked himself in his own campaign ads ("I'm not a fancy talker") won the election and became mayor in his own right.

"I never saw myself as mayor of Boston—even before I became acting mayor!" Menino laughs as we speak in his city hall office during the waning days of his final term. "My book's not gonna say, 'When I was four years old, I dreamed of becoming mayor of Boston.' I didn't dream about it till I was forty-eight years old!"

As mayor, Menino found his footing as a popular and effective leader. In time, the derisive nicknames ("Mumbles," "Accidental Mayor") faded away as surely as did close elections for Tom Menino, who ultimately served an unprecedented five terms over twenty years, a record in Boston's 375-year history, and one not likely to be repeated. Moreover, had health issues not forced him to forego running again in 2013, it's likely he would have won an extraordinary sixth term.

"And I don't think they would have counted his votes," says Brett, shaking his head. "They would have weighed them."

The one nickname Menino embraced—"Mayor Pothole"—appealed to him precisely because it summed up what seemed to be the essence of his political philosophy: "Focus on stuff people need; fix stuff people use." No meeting or group gathering was too minor for Menino; nearing the end of his tenure, it was said that more than half of the city's residents had met the mayor personally at least once over the years.

"It's very difficult," observes Larry DiCara, "to vote against someone who personally calls you up on the phone and says, 'I know you have a problem with a streetlight on Elm Street—it'll be fixed tomorrow.'"

But as beloved as Menino became for his tirelessness and single-minded focus on his city, he was also feared for his thin skin, quick temper, and a tendency to hold onto grudges. Tenaciously. Permanently.

"I once described his skin as being 'prosciutto-thin,'" says long-time *Boston Globe* columnist Joan Vennochi. "One very early morning at my house, the phone rang and it was Tom Menino, expressing his distaste for my opinion in that morning's *Globe*. And I thought to myself, Don't you have a city to run?"

It was said that crossing Menino could doom the project or proposal of anyone who had business before the city. One local developer, having aroused Menino's ire, spent years feuding publicly with him over a proposed building on the waterfront.

"Menino has had the last word on that," observes Vennochi.

Last word, indeed. Thomas M. Menino died in 2014. The developer is still pushing his proposal.

At the same time, some of Menino's most publicized feuds were not a result of thin skin, but deep values. Like fairness and equality.

When gays and lesbians were barred from marching by organizers of South Boston's annual St. Patrick's Day parade, Menino broke with longstanding tradition and refused to march. He never marched there again.

"For a man who loves to march in parades? In a part of the city with the highest voter turnout?" marvels DiCara. "That was an act of true political courage."

And, in Southie, anyway, an act of political suicide. (In 2015, a year after Menino died, the South Boston St. Patrick's Day parade welcomed LBGT groups to march.)

Such is the turbulent and tribal nature of Boston's highly localized turf wars and political feuds. Indeed, Tom Menino was far from unique in having a long memory when it came to keeping score politically. In Boston politics, it simply goes with the territory.

"I had total recall for people who were with me, and total recall for people who screwed me," says Larry DiCara. "I still remember who voted for me for class president in 1966 at Boston Latin!"

Boston. The home of the bean and the cod. And where you're either with me or against me.

"Neighbors would go against neighbors—that was always tough," says Jim Brett. "People would be walking at Castle Island (South Boston); guy would say, 'Hey, there's Tom Foley,' and his friend would say, 'Yeah, but he wasn't with us.' *Wasn't with us.* That was the code word."

Few politicians in Boston's history understood the codes better than former mayors John F. ("Honey Fitz") Fitzgerald and James Michael Curley. Ironically, while the two men ultimately figured in perhaps the city's nastiest feud of all, they had much in common, and were surprisingly alike in many ways. Both were first-generation Americans, born in Boston to hardworking Irish-Catholic immigrants. Each had a passion and a gift for politics, but began their

James Michael Curley, 1914 LIBRARY OF CONGRESS

respective careers in a city that still tilted heavily Protestant politically, and still harbored a deep prejudice to newcomers in general, and the Irish in particular. But gradually, by dint of sheer numbers, the tide began to change.

"If you were poor or a minority, people figured out that elective office could be a way up and out and onto a rung of the ladder," says DiCara. "Honey Fitz and Curley were both very poor, and for both of them, it was a way up and out and meant advancement."

And advance Fitzgerald did. Elected first to Boston's Common Council in 1891, he then won a state senate seat and by 1895 was representing the Massachusetts Ninth District in the U.S. Congress. In 1906, he became Boston's first American-born, Irish-Catholic mayor, and served two terms, from 1906 to 1908, and from 1910 to 1914.

Writing about Fitzgerald, the historian Robert Dallek described him as "a natural politician—a charming, impish, affable lover of people." He could just as easily have described James Michael Curley.

With a father who was a small-time crook, Curley worked his way up through an even harder school of hard knocks than Fitzgerald. (Who, it should be noted, endured terrible family tragedies as well.) In a peculiar turn of events that would be repeated, Curley won his first election (Boston's Board of Aldermen) while serving time in prison for fraud. (He and a friend were caught taking a civil service exam to help two other men from their ward get jobs.) It gave Curley a criminal record, but it also gave him a lifelong reputation, mostly among the city's Irish voters, as a modern-day Robin Hood type of politician, who would rise up the ladder, but never forget to help those on the lower rungs. In truth, mirroring each other again, neither Curley nor Fitzgerald had any trouble remembering where they came from. What both often managed to forget about were annoying little details like rules, ethics, and other assorted legalities.

(For example . . . Curley was a regular visitor to Boston's storied Irish pub, Doyle's, where former owner Gerry Burke shared with me his favorite Curley story: The late mayor had built a mansion for himself alongside the city's scenic Jamaica Pond. One day, he set himself up in a back room at Doyle's in order to "interview" potential candidates to paint the new house. Suitor after suitor was ushered in to ask for the job. Finally, a very nervous, just-off-the-boat Irishman, hat-in-hand, knelt before Curley and breathlessly exclaimed, "Yer Honor, it would be my pleasure to paint yer house fer nuthin'!"

"For *nothing*?" Curley exploded indignantly. "Is that the best you can do?")

In 1910 Curley won a congressional seat from the Tenth District. Four years later, he won his first of four terms as mayor of Boston. (None of the terms were consecutive and, more remarkably, were spread out over five decades, between 1914 and 1950.) But the mayoral campaign of 1914 was particularly noteworthy. It signaled both Curley's triumphant arrival and Fitzgerald's unpleasant and untimely exit.

All tied up in an unsightly bow of treachery that would itself reach across decades.

Although Fitzgerald, then fifty, had earlier signaled he might not run for reelection, the inconvenient and frustrating fact in 1913 for the hard-charging, thirty-nine-year-old James Michael Curley was that incumbent Honey Fitz had then decided to run after all. At some point during this period of time, the Curley campaign, through an outside source, was provided with some highly personal and potentially very damaging information regarding Fitzgerald. The information alleged that Fitzgerald had been seen, by multiple witnesses, dancing and carrying on with a twenty-three-year-old showgirl at a suburban Boston roadhouse. The young woman's nickname was "Toodles," thus providing the Curley campaign with only one of several elements about the story that proved to be politically irresistible.

Returning to his Dorchester home one evening, Fitzgerald encountered his wife, Josephine, and his daughter, Rose, waiting for him. They had already read a letter that had been delivered to the house earlier that day. It threatened to make the "Toodles" information public unless Fitzgerald withdrew immediately from the mayoral race. In his definitive biography on Curley, *The Rascal King*, author Jack Beatty describes the scene: "John Fitzgerald had opened his door that evening to find his wife and his eldest daughter, Rose (who, like Toodles, was twenty-three), waiting for him in the hallway. He later told a friend that it was the worst moment of his life. Josephine had insisted that he comply with the letter's demand."

While Fitzgerald claimed that the contents of the letter were untrue, and pleaded to be allowed to fight it, he ultimately complied with his wife's—and the letter's—demand, and withdrew from the race.

Blackmail accomplished, Curley cruised to victory in November. The incident, however, would reverberate decades later. Rose Fitzgerald was, after all, the future mother of a future American president, whose guiding political maxim would be, "Don't get mad; get even." And he would.

Following his first victory as mayor, Curley's colorful and kaleidoscopic career unfolded in seemingly endless installments. Not content (like Tom Menino) to be a mere big-city mayor, Curley's ceaseless political ambitions frequently overran starker political realities. Beloved by Boston's Irish community and much of its

Mayor John F. "Honey Fitz" Fitzgerald, greeting Boston Braves star Hank Gowdy, 1914 LIBRARY OF CONGRESS

working class, he was viewed far less positively in other quarters of the voting public. He ran unsuccessfully for a U.S. Senate seat (FDR, a fellow Democrat, declined to endorse him), as well as the Massachusetts governorship, before winning that office in 1934. He won two other terms as mayor, but also lost mayoral elections in 1937 and 1940. In 1941, he did reclaim a U.S. congressional seat, this time from the Eleventh District. (A seat that was to become richly upholstered in irony.)

In 1946, Curley began his fourth and what would become his final term as mayor of Boston. But his fast and easy way with money and the law was about to catch up with him. Indeed, he had won the election in 1945 even in the face of a federal felony indictment. But the hammer finally dropped in 1946, when he was convicted of

Curley returns to Boston, 1936. PHOTO, COURTESY OF THE TRUSTEES OF THE BOSTON
PUBLIC LIBRARY/LESLIE JONES COLLECTION

mail fraud, and sentenced to a term at the federal prison in Danbury, Connecticut. Back in Boston, where corruption was clearly no career killer, laws were changed to allow for a harmless (or so it was assumed) placeholder to occupy the mayor's chair until his eventual return.

And, just to grease the skids, a petition was circulated, asking President Truman to grant clemency to Curley. It was signed by hundreds of members of the U.S. House, including every member of the Massachusetts congressional delegation, with one notable exception: the newly elected Democratic congressman from Curley's old Eleventh District, now represented by none other than Honey Fitz's grandson, thirty-year-old John Fitzgerald Kennedy.

June, 1946: Former Mayor John F. Fitzgerald with grandson, soon-to-be Congressman, and future U.S. President, John F. Kennedy. (JFK's father, Joseph P. Kennedy, looks on.) PHOTO, HY PESKIN/LOOK MAGAZINE/JOHN F. KENNEDY PRESIDENTIAL LIBRARY AND MUSEUM

Refusing to forget what Curley had done to his grandfather, JFK refused to sign the ailing mayor's petition. *Don't get mad; get even.*

Truman did end up commuting Curley's sentence, but that could not stem a more punishing verdict awaiting the mayor. He was soundly defeated in his bid for a fifth term (inspiration for the book and film *The Last Hurrah*) and, at seventy-six and in ill health, was forced to accept that he'd reached his political finish line. Embittered, he died in 1958.

Two mayors: John F. Fitzgerald (left) and James Michael Curley PHOTO, COURTESY OF THE TRUSTEES OF THE BOSTON PUBLIC LIBRARY/LESLIE JONES COLLECTION

But in Boston, history can be a fluid thing. It's everywhere, and the past frequently seems to waft up and insinuate itself in the present. After his descendants had disappeared from politics one by one, many tragically, Honey Fitz's great-great grandson (Joseph Kennedy III) now represents the Massachusetts Fourth District in the U.S. Congress. At Boston City Hall, the view from the mayor's office down to those statues below now belongs to Martin J. Walsh, elected in 2013. Soon after taking office, Walsh, the city's fifty-fourth mayor, retrieved a specific desk for his use in city hall. It had been gone for decades. But then, so had its original owner, James Michael Curley. In Boston politics, even the ghosts can make a comeback.

CHAPTER 7

Po(e)stscript

With few exceptions, all of the feuds described in this book are ongoing. In some cases, they've been going on for centuries—the principals long deceased, but the points of contention alive and well, and the feud never to end.

And then, lo and behold, one does. In a way.

Not only that, but this was a feud that was as colorful and long-standing as any you could find in New England. And it came to a close just as I was researching and writing this book.

To be accurate, only one party in this case was actually involved in burying the hatchet. The other party—fittingly known as "Tomahawk man"—has been dead for 166 years.

In the early to mid-nineteenth century, the Boston area was home to such legendary literary figures as Nathaniel Hawthorne, Ralph Waldo Emerson, Louisa May Alcott, and Henry Wadsworth Longfellow. It was also home to Edgar Allan Poe, who had little regard for any of those writers. The fact that the feeling was mostly mutual accounts for one of America's most notable and nasty literary feuds.

Edgar Allan Poe was born in Boston in 1809. His parents' house (long gone) stood on the edge of the city's South End, in a neighborhood of the city known today as Bay Village. His early, sad childhood perhaps prefigures (accounts for?) the dark works for which he himself became legendary. Born to two actors (two strikes right there), his father abandoned the family a year after Poe was born; his mother died a year later. So much for a happy childhood. But so much material to work with.

Poe was taken in by a couple in Virginia, with whom he lived until he went off to a year of college, which didn't take. (Hey, it didn't initially for me, either.) What had taken hold, though, was a passionate love of poetry, and writing. In 1827, after a brief stint in the army, Poe had his first collection of poems, *Tamerlane and Other Poems*, published. Although he had not lived in Boston for nearly twenty years, Poe signed his first published work simply, "a Bostonian." This suggests an enduring fondness for his birth city, even as his budding professional life as a writer, editor, and critic (sometimes a particularly savage one, hence the "Tomahawk" nickname) took him to live in New York, Philadelphia, and Baltimore.

Poe did occasionally return to Boston. But it was clear that his emerging personal style was in stark and striking contrast with the more rarified sensibility of the city's literary establishment. In addition, the 1830s in Boston were marked by the burgeoning Transcendentalist movement. Inspired by Unitarianism, Transcendentalism influenced popular culture, religion, philosophy, and literature. Leading literary figures and intellectuals like Ralph Waldo Emerson and Henry David Thoreau helped popularize it. These men— and the wider Boston literary and intellectual community of the time—devoted much of their writing to the great, contemporary social issues, like the abolition of slavery. As writers and thinkers go, lofty is a word that seems to fit Emerson. It did not fit Poe. As a writer, he seemed to recoil from it, believing instead that successful writing should aim to entertain, not inspire or spread a message.

"He who pleases is of more importance to his fellow man than he who instructs," Poe wrote.

As time went on, and as he wielded a more and more public pen, Poe took increasing delight in mocking what he saw as a Boston literary style of stuffy, high-minded, and pretentious moralism, versus simply telling a good story that appealed to the broader culture. He taunted Boston's biggest and best-known literary and public figures. He called them, "Frogpondians," comparing their puffed-up and incessant intellectual and philosophical "croaking" to the sound one might hear from the Frog Pond on Boston Common. But really, his distaste for all things Boston extended to the city as a whole.

"They have no soul," wrote Poe, describing Bostonians. "Well-bred, as very dull persons very generally are."

In turn, the Boston literary elite derided Poe with equal relish. Of Poe's signature poem, "The Raven," Emerson wrote, "I see nothing in it."

And so the feud continued, for years, until Poe's death, in Baltimore, in 1849.

In 2009, the Boston Public Library held an exhibit titled, "The Raven in the Frog Pond," which chronicled Poe's lifelong quarrel with his birthplace. Paul Lewis, a Boston College English professor and Poe scholar, curated the exhibit and makes the case that this feud, however nasty, ultimately helped shape and sharpen Poe's persona and priorities as a writer, and helped define how we see him today.

"Poe knew he was, among other things, a pen and ink scribbler trying to keep up in a changing marketplace," says Lewis in a phone conversation. "And the Transcendentalists knew what they were about—personal growth and social reform."

What's more, Lewis argues, Poe ultimately prevailed.

"The quarrel is really about literature and pop culture—and Poe won!" says Lewis. "The Transcendentalist message is not filling the multiplexes—Poe is. He triumphed over them."

Perhaps. But until recently, it was those whom Poe supposedly triumphed over—Emerson, Thoreau, and others—who nonetheless have statues of themselves in Greater Boston and other memorials to honor them. But not Poe. The Boston Public Library exhibit points out that in each of the other East Coast cities in which Poe lived and worked for a time (Richmond, Philadelphia, Baltimore, New York), some type of museum or memorial to Poe exists. By contrast, as Paul Lewis wrote for the exhibit, "Boston has made itself conspicuous for its apparent determination to treat the master of mystery—America's first great critic and a foundational figure in the development of popular culture—like an undeserving orphan."

And so it seemed to stay that way. A small square and a street near Poe's birthplace in Boston bore his name. But that was pretty much it. In fairness, as Lewis himself points out, it did not seem to be any lingering hostility on the city's part; more simple neglect and lack of any focused effort to do something.

"It would be a mistake," Lewis told me, "to think that since the middle of the nineteenth-century, Bostonians in general disliked Poe—not true."

But neither did Boston do much to embrace Poe—who was, after all, born there. ("One of the best-kept secrets in Boston's literary history!" observes the BPL exhibit's introduction.)

That finally changed, beginning in 2009 with the bicentennial of Poe's birth. In Boston, a genuine desire took hold to finally forget

Edgar Allan Poe LIBRARY OF CONGRESS

the quarrels of the past and honor Poe. Just blocks from the site of Poe's former home, a site was selected for a significant statue. A sculptor was chosen. So was a theme: This was a memorial meant to have special meaning in the city where it would stand. And only there.

"The city made it clear that they wanted to reference Poe's complicated relationship with Boston," sculptor Stefanie Rocknak tells me. "They made it clear that the work was to be very Boston-specific."

And so it is. Rocknak's sculpture portrays a full-size Poe, coat open and flowing in the wind, as he seems to hurry along the

Edgar Allan Poe returns to Boston. PHOTO, COURTESY OF STEFANIE ROCKNAK

sidewalk with great purpose. In what could be regarded as a final gesture now literally set in stone, his back is to Boston Common and the fabled Frog Pond.

"I definitely wanted to capture Poe's conflicted relationship with Boston," says Rocknak, a Maine native, who now teaches at Hartwick College in Oneonta, New York. "He never fully belonged there, so he is walking away from the Frog Pond, and walking toward where he was born."

In addition, Rocknak's Poe is carrying an overflowing valise that reveals symbols synonymous with Poe—a human heart, and an oversized raven taking flight. Papers flow out behind him.

"He's sort of making, or leaving, his mark in Boston," Rocknak says.

Finally.

On October 5, 2014, Rocknak's statue was officially dedicated in Boston.

"It's time that Poe, whose hometown was Boston, be honored for his connection to the city," said Boston Mayor Martin J. Walsh.

And with that, in bright sunshine that seemed decidedly un-Poe-like, Rocknak's statue was unveiled. Today, visitors often stop at it to take selfies, sometimes draping an arm around a man who spent his life holding the city at arm's length. Now, Boston seems to be saying, "Forget all that—gimme a hug!"

"He's home," says Rocknak.

Finally. Feuds rarely end easily, or quickly, if they end at all. But sometimes they do end.

Even if, ultimately, it's in absentia.

"It only took 165 years," notes Paul Lewis, wryly.

But who's counting?

Acknowledgments

I must say thanks—first, last, and always—to my wife, Anne-Marie, and my daughters, Kyra and Daisy. Their patience, understanding, and support make all the difference in getting a long, arduous project like this done. I, in turn, tried to keep my absences to a minimum, and most importantly, we've all managed to avoid any feuds of our own from rivaling any in this book.

Thanks also to those at WCVB-TV and *Chronicle* whose support also has meant so much: general manager Bill Fine, *Chronicle* executive producer Chris Stirling, and managing editor Susan Sloane. Thanks as well at WCVB to Leona McCarthy, graphics designer Bryan Kelleher, editor Gino Mauro, longtime colleague and producer Clint Conley, and equally longtime *Chronicle* photographer and friend Carl Vieira.

At Globe Pequot, I continue to be so grateful to editor Erin Turner, ever wise, helpful, and patient, who never fails to answer my many questions, no matter how dumb, and who always adds unexpected information to my day by telling me how the weather is outside her window in Montana. Thanks also at GP to Ellen Urban, Sharon Kunz, and Amy Alexander.

A note of thanks as well to the following institutions: the alumni office of Major League Baseball, the Baseball Hall of Fame in Cooperstown, New York, the Library of Congress, the Collections Department of the Boston Public Library, and the John Fitzgerald Kennedy Museum and Library in Boston. And, not least, to the following individuals: John Brown, Andy Kosch, John Shannahan,

Diane Heileman, and Josh Pahigian. And a special thanks to my old friend, Chris Russell. Thank you all.

Most of all, I am so grateful to all of those who gave their time and voices and personal recollections in sharing the stories that are in this book, and in helping me tell them. Just two examples—Bill Lee's irreverent humor and Goose Gossage's crusty good cheer— were reason enough to make me wonder sometimes what all that feuding was all about, anyway.

Thank you all.

ABOUT THE AUTHOR

Ted Reinstein has been a reporter for *Chronicle*, WCVB-TV/ Boston's award-winning—and America's longest-running, locally produced—nightly news magazine since 1997. In addition, he is a regular contributor for the station's political roundtable show, and sits on the station's editorial board. He is also the author of *New England Notebook: One Reporter, Six States, Uncommon Stories* (Globe Pequot, 2013). He lives just west of Boston with his wife and two daughters.